Palmerston Ontario in Colour Photos, Saving Our History One Photo at a Time

I0484342

Photography
by Barbara Raué
2014

Series Name:
Cruising Ontario

Book 76: Palmerston

Cover photo: Main Street house

Series Name: Cruising Ontario
Saving Our History One Photo at a Time

Other Books by Barbara Raue

Coins of Gold

Arrows, Indians and Love

The Life and Times of Barbara
Volume 1: Inventions That Have Enhanced My Life
Volume 2: Entertainment That I Have Enjoyed
Volume 3: East Coast Trips
Volume 4: Olympics Have Always Intrigued Me
Volume 5: Wonders of the World
Volume 6: Caribbean Cruises We Have Enjoyed
Volume 7: Animals
Volume 8: Storms and Other Major Disasters in My Lifetime
Volume 9: Wars, Terrorist Attacks and Major Disasters

The Cromwell Family Book

Laura Secord Discovered

Visit Barbara's website to view all of her books
http://barbararaue.ca

Palmerston

Palmerston is located in Wellington County, west of Arthur, northeast of Listowel, and northwest of Kitchener and Waterloo.

The opening in 1871 of a station on the main line of the Wellington, Grey and Bruce Railway soon to be completed from Guelph to Southampton, provided the nucleus around which a community developed. In its original concept the railroad was to run from Guelph to Harriston and would not have gone through Palmerston. Listowel needed to be linked to the railroad and it was decided to bend the route toward Listowel. It was also decided that a yard with maintenance shops would be needed. As soon as the railroad decided where it would build, people started buying property around the area for businesses and homes.

Thomas McDowell was the first settler in 1854 on the site. In 1872 McDowell and William Thompson who owned adjoining land, began selling town lots and by 1873 the community had 150 inhabitants.

In 1873 a branch line to Listowel was completed and a post office called Palmerston, named after Lord Palmerston, a celebrated English statesman, was opened.

Table of Contents

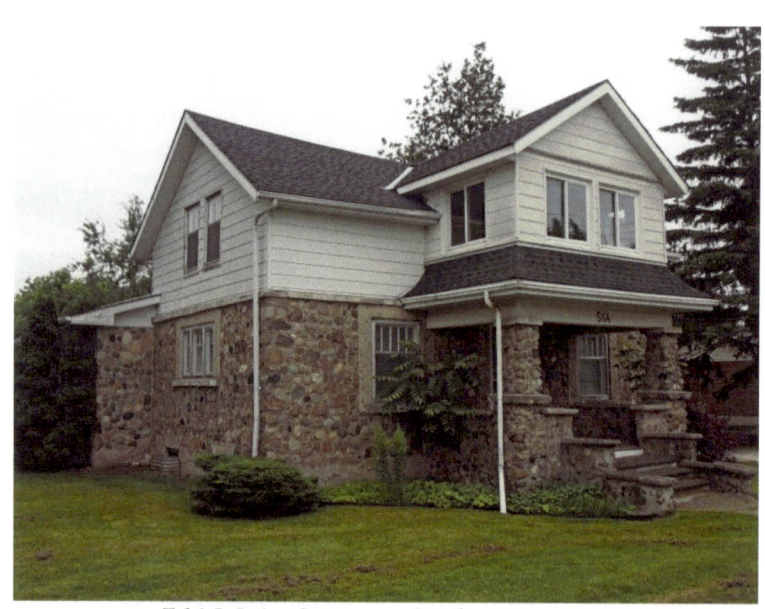

564 Main Street – Gothic Revival

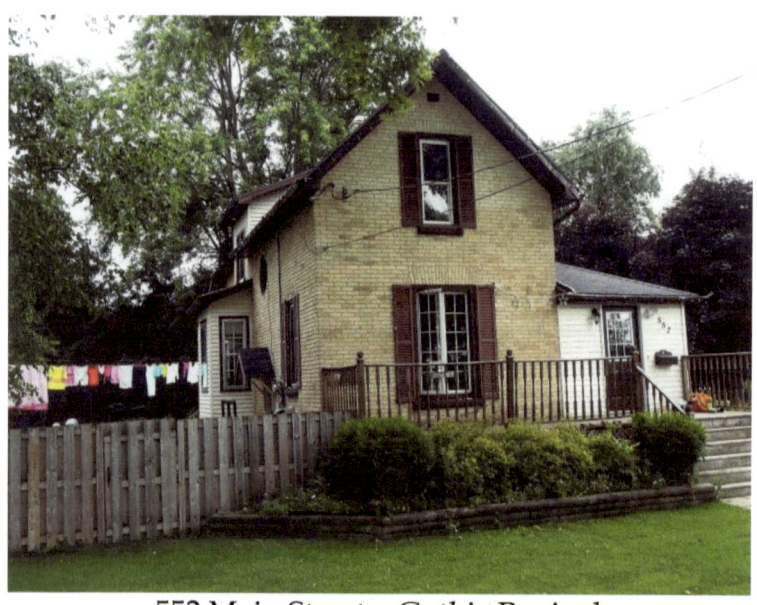

552 Main Street – Gothic Revival

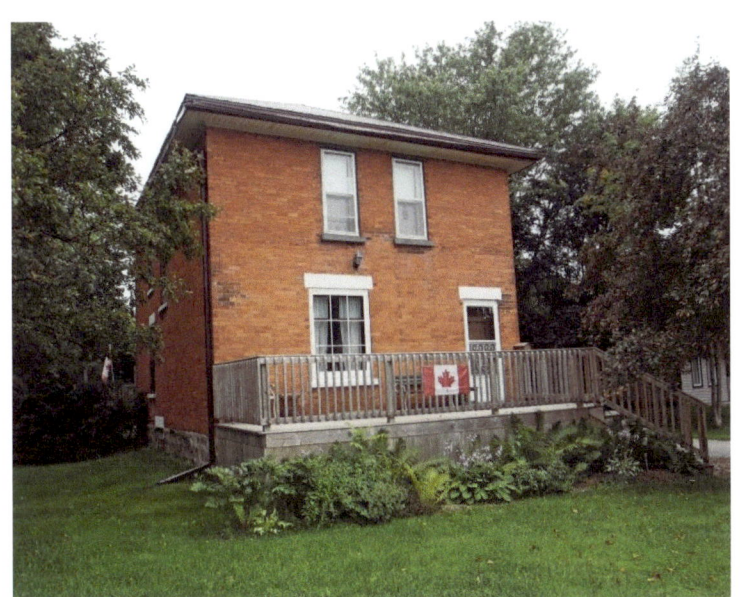

Main Street – Italianate – hipped roof

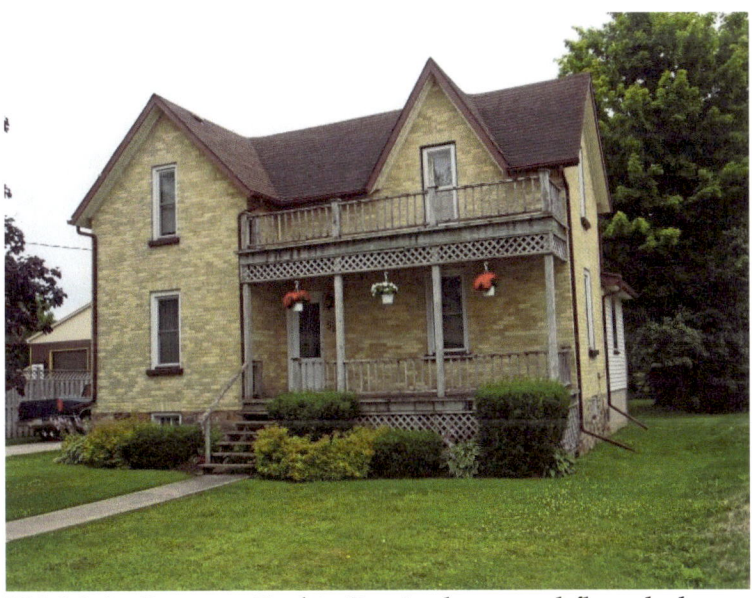

520 Main Street – Gothic Revival, second floor balcony

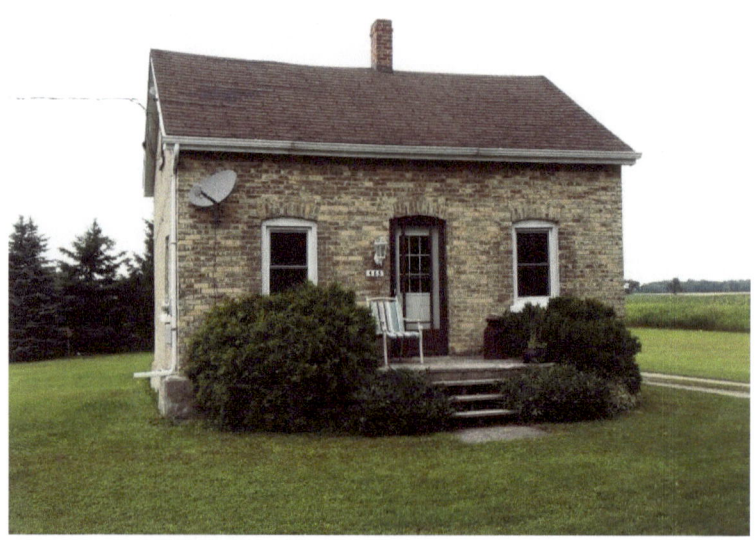

485 Main Street – Gothic Revival

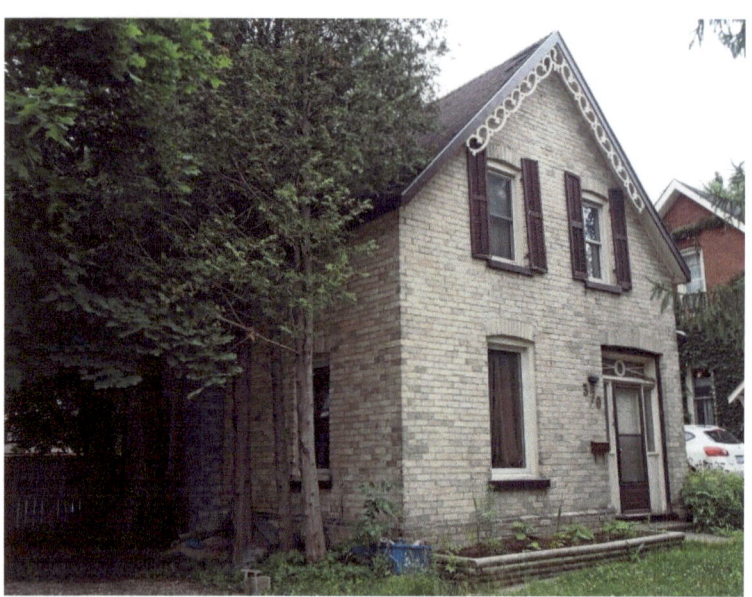

370 Main Street – Gothic Revival – Vergeboard trim

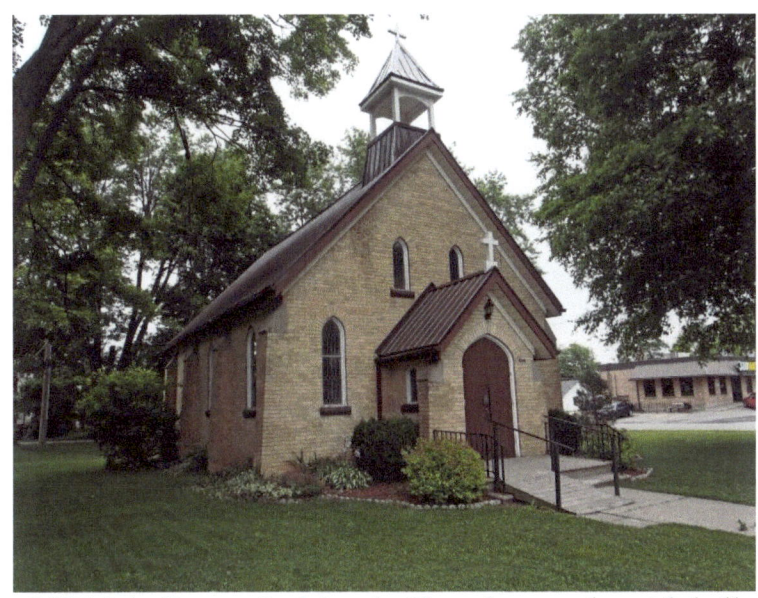

365 Main Street, St. Mary's Church, cupola with bell

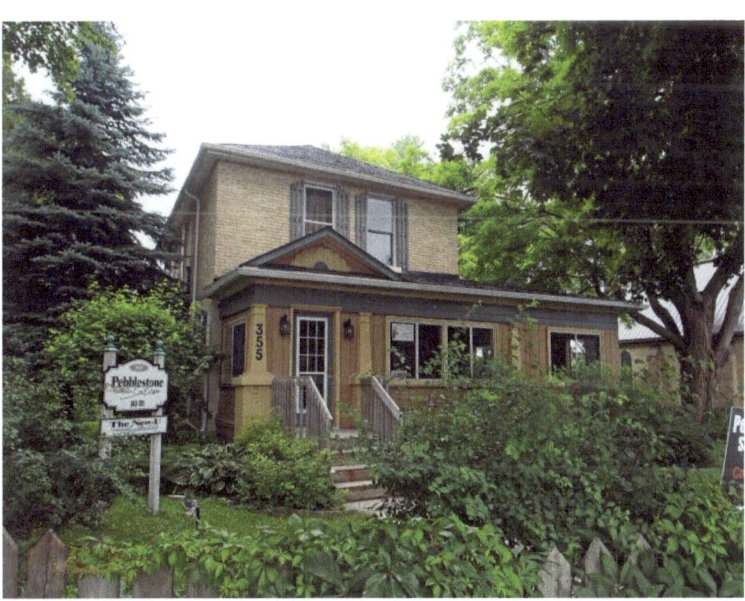

355 Main Street – Italianate – hipped roof, with added enclosed front porch

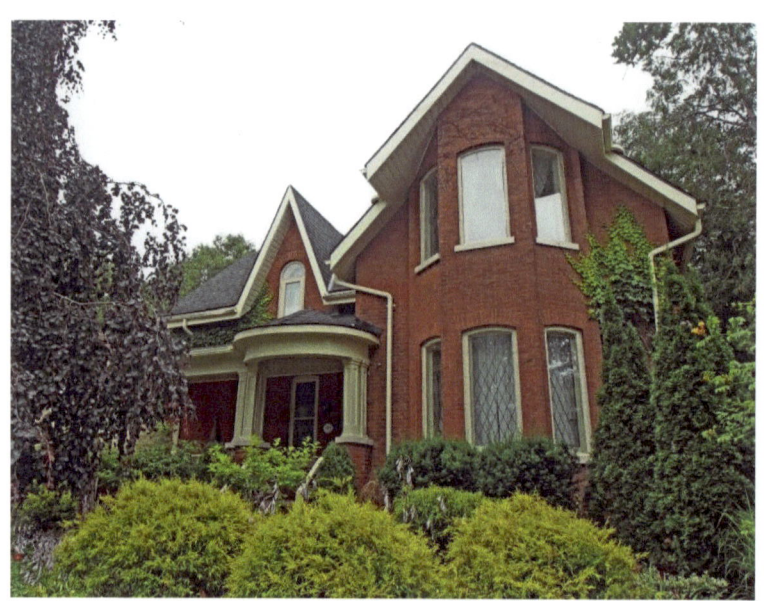

350 Main Street – Gothic Revival

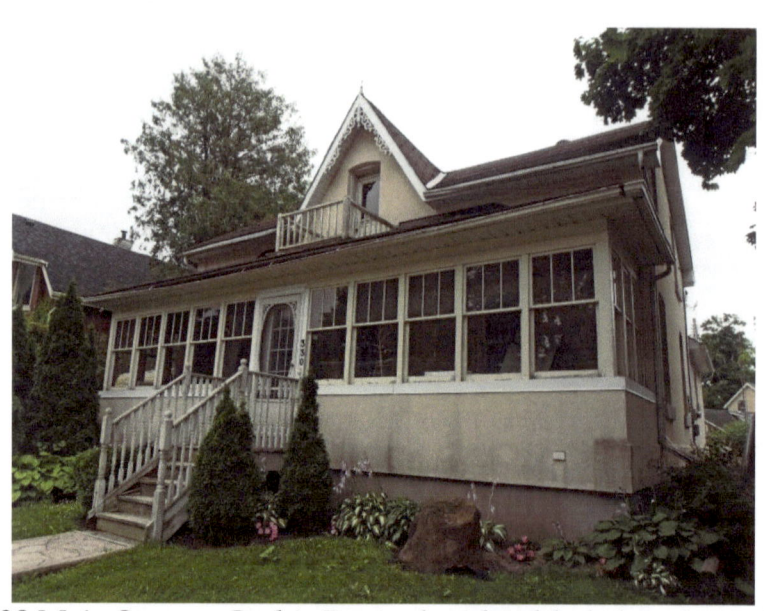

330 Main Street – Gothic Revival with added closed porch, Vergeboard trim and finial on gable

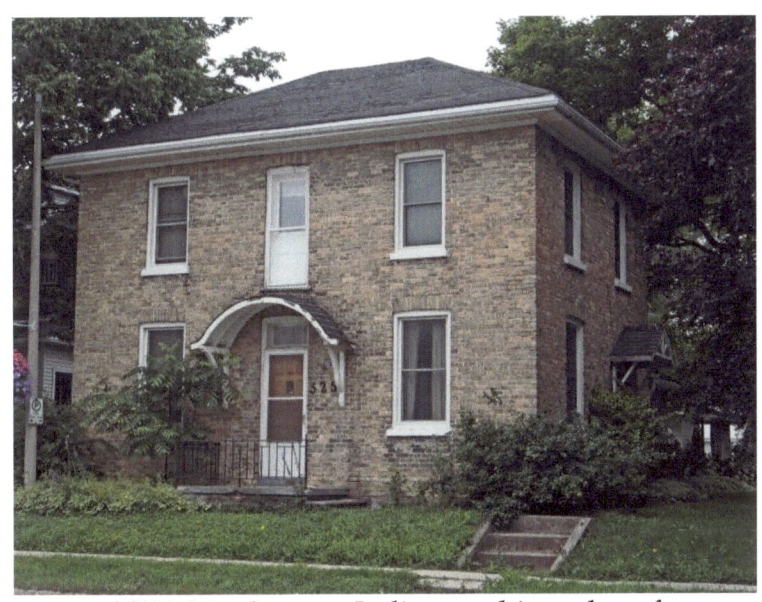

325 Main Street – Italianate, hipped roof

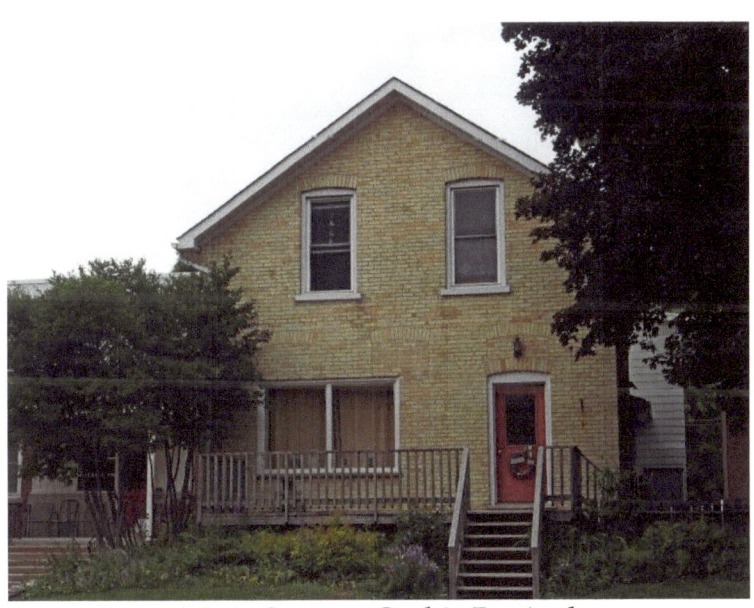

Main Street – Gothic Revival

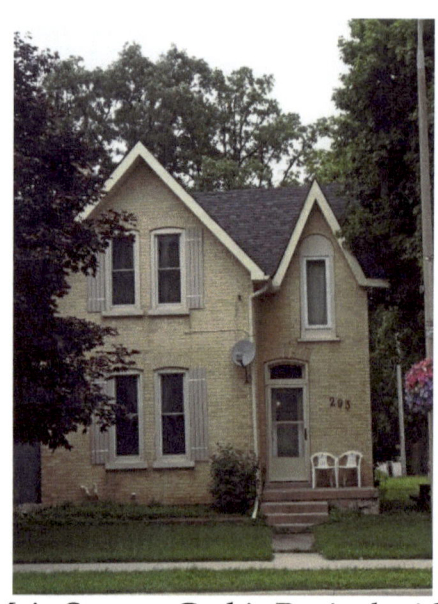

293 Main Street – Gothic Revival with two gables

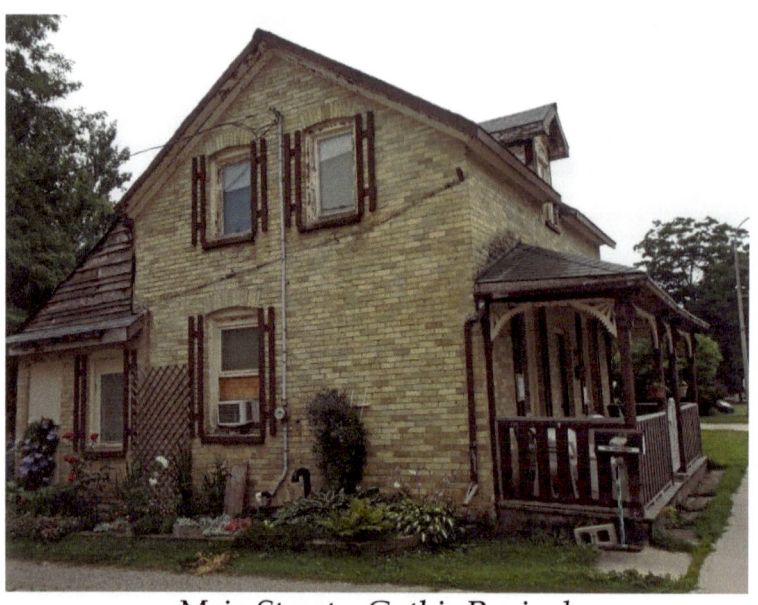

Main Street – Gothic Revival

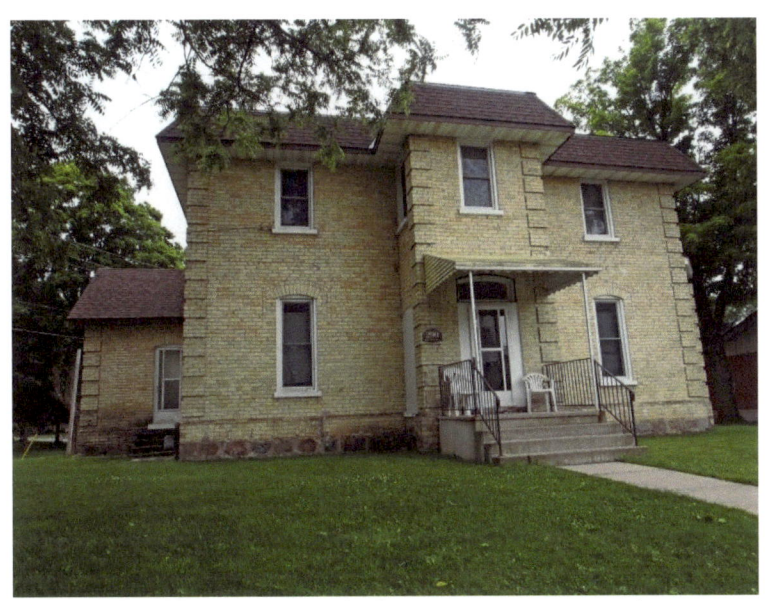

290 Main Street – Italianate, corner quoins

The Ontario Vaccine Farm was established in 1885 by Dr. Alexander Stewart, a local physician. It was the first institution to produce smallpox vaccine in Ontario. The Farm originally consisted of a converted barn where Stewart employed government-approved methods for obtaining and processing vaccine from inoculated calves. During an era of recurring smallpox outbreaks in Ontario, large quantities were sold to local health boards for preventative vaccination. By 1907, although American farms were supplying most of the vaccine used in Ontario, Stewart had constructed new buildings, including a combined operating room and laboratory. After Stewart's death in 1911, the operation was continued by Dr. H. B. Coleman until 1916 when it was taken over by and transferred to the Antitoxin Laboratory of the University of Toronto.

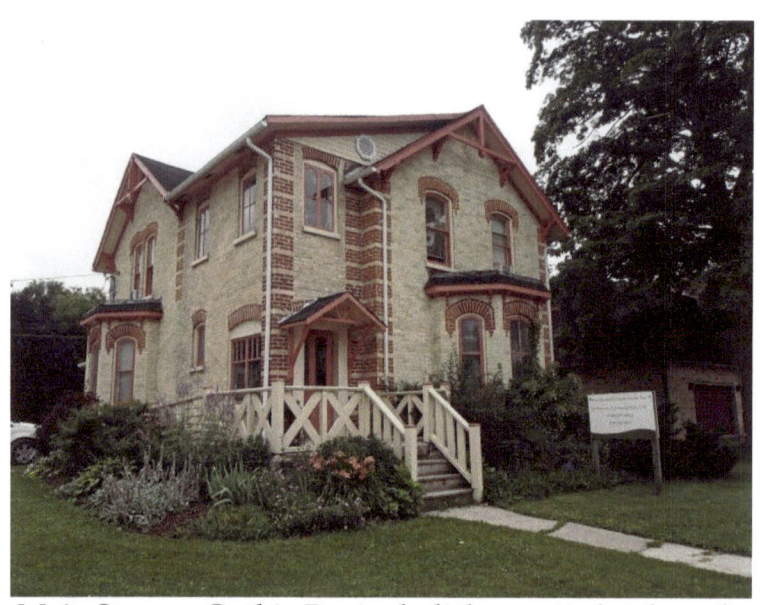

Main Street – Gothic Revival, dichromatic brickwork,
bay windows, corner quoins

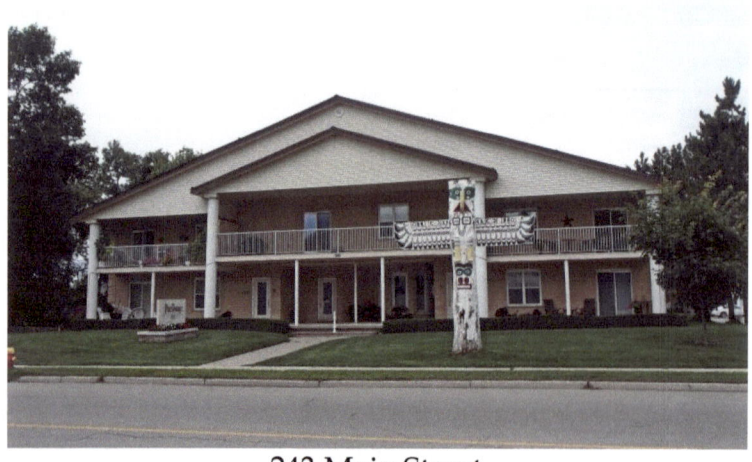

243 Main Street

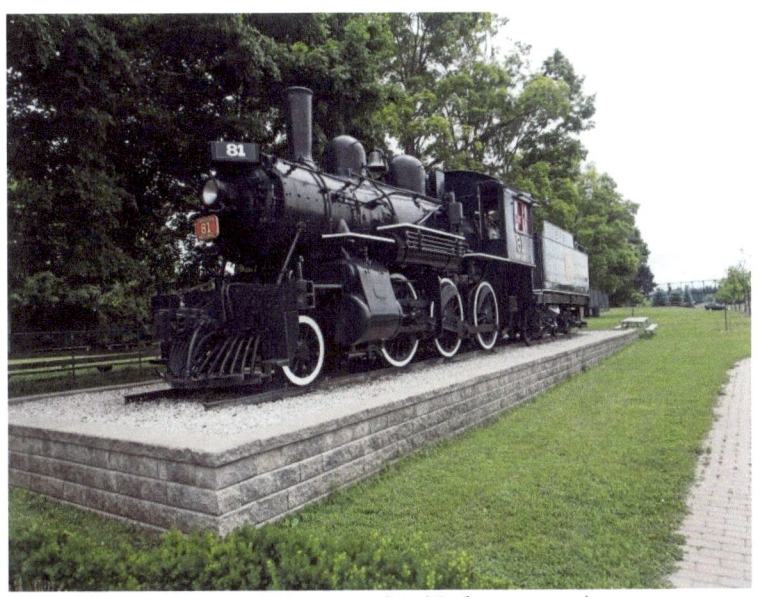

Steam Engine #81 (Palmerston)
This coal-burner was built by the Canadian Locomotion
Company (Kingston) in 1910. It was designed for passenger
service and it could haul 10 to 12 passenger coaches. This
mogul type engine (2 front – six driving wheels) was built for
the Grand Trunk Railway.
#81 was retired from service January 29, 1957.
It was restored in 2008 to honour the heritage of Palmerston.

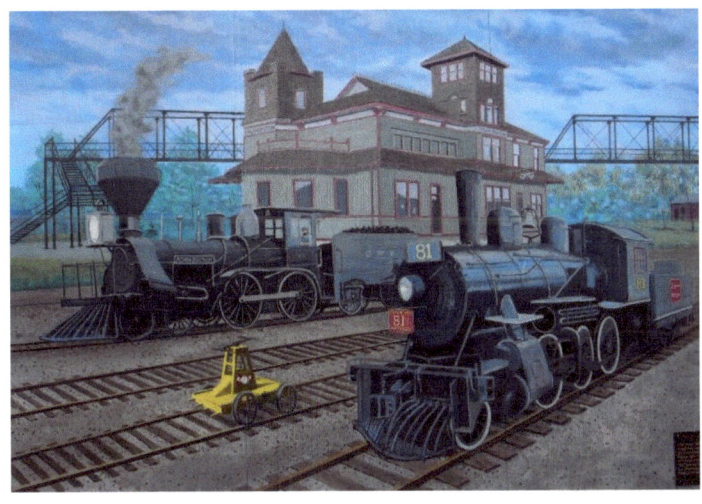

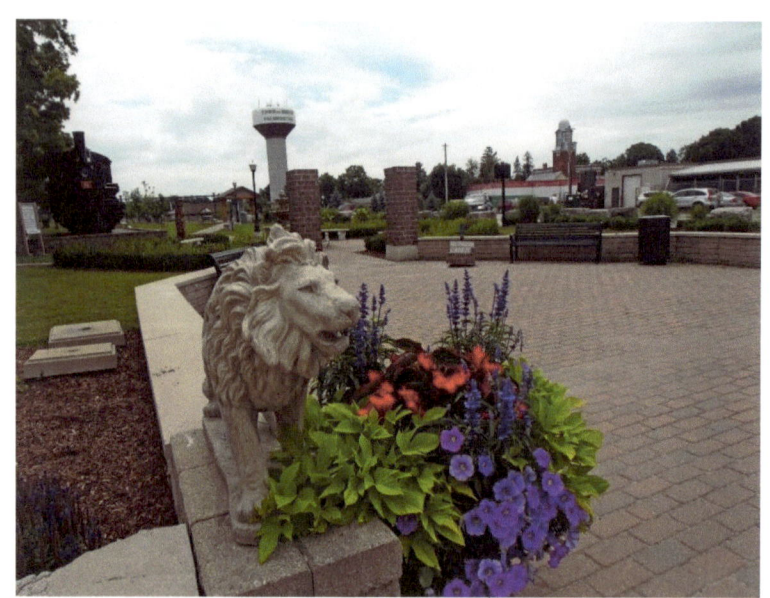

Lion guarding the park

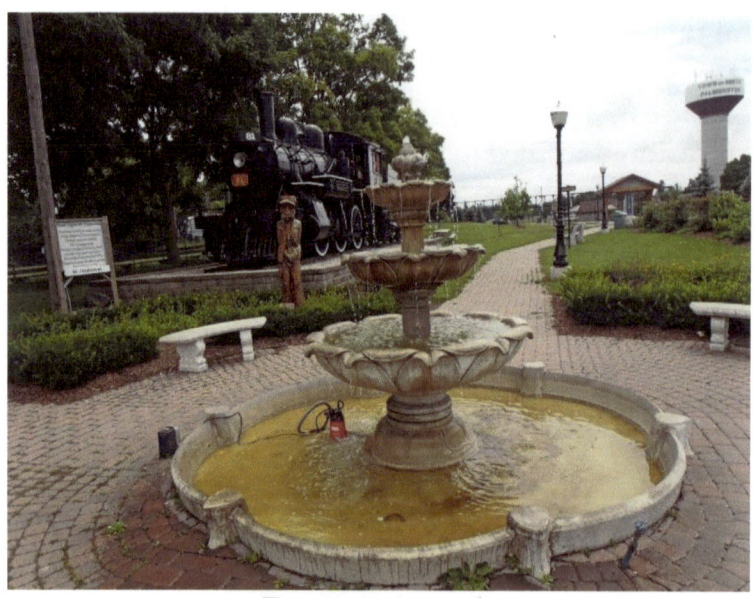

Fountain in park

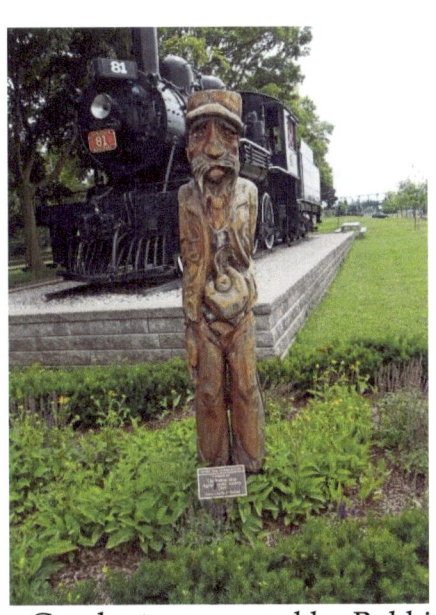

Spike the Conductor – carved by Bobbi Switzer

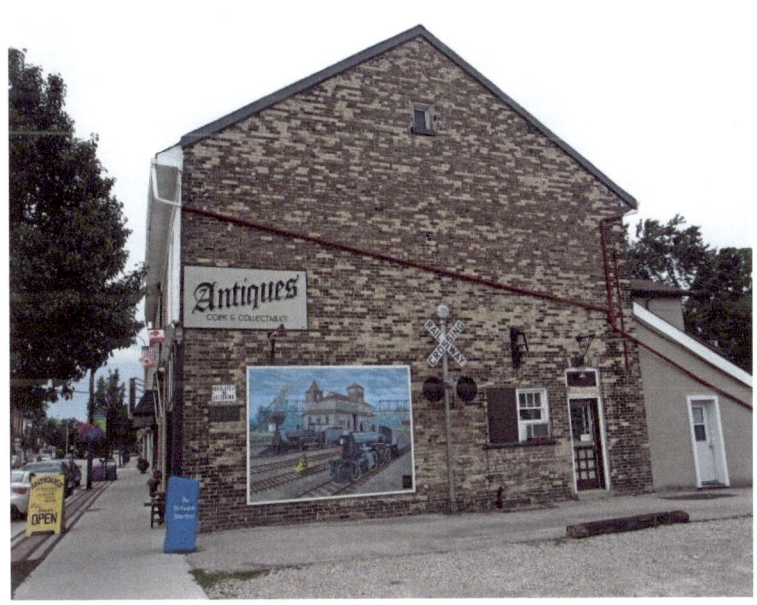

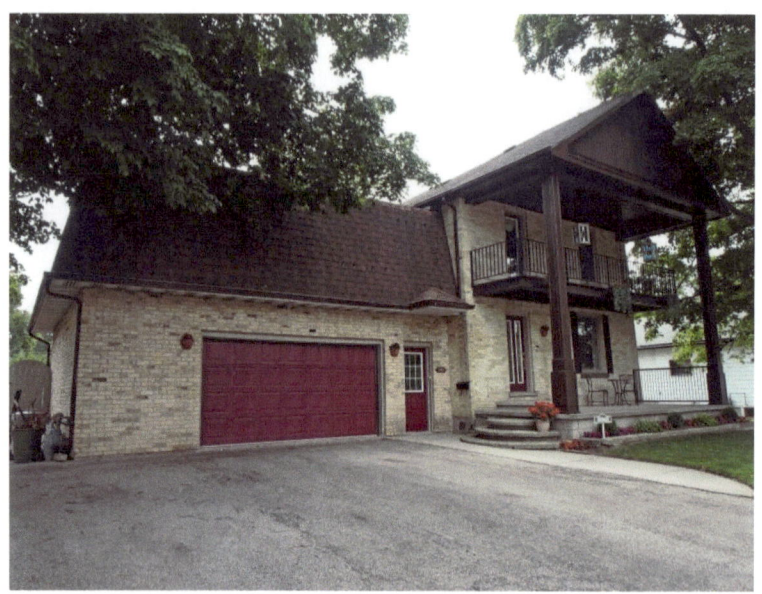

140 Main Street

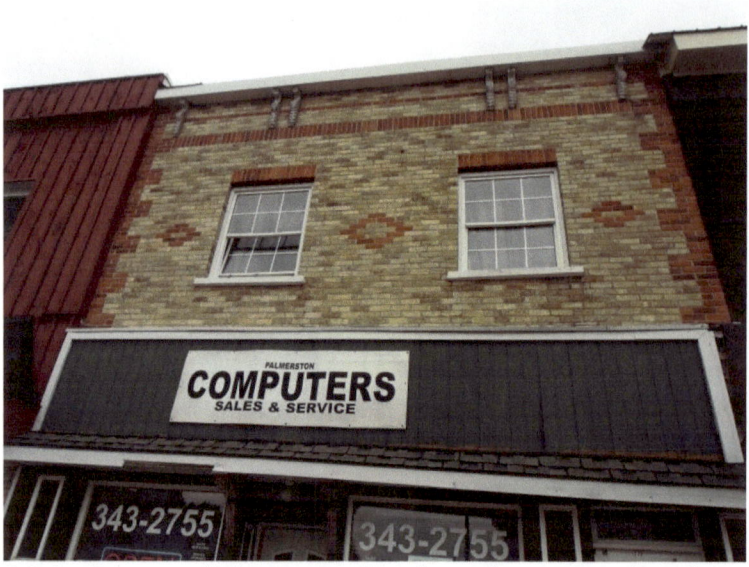

Main Street – dichromatic brickwork, cornice brackets

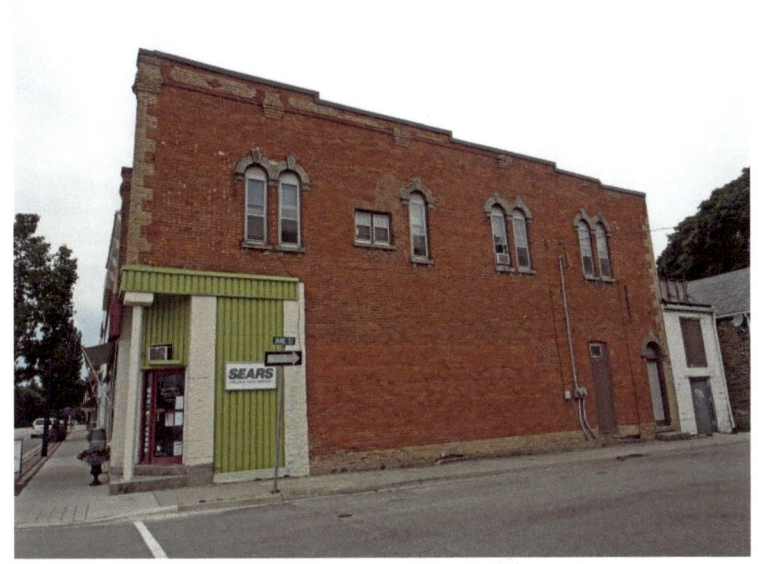

Corner quoin, voussoirs and keystones

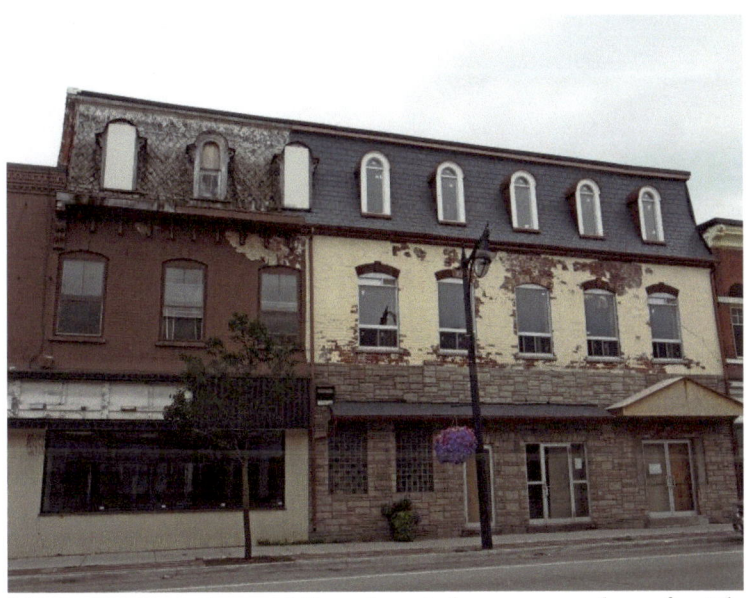

Main Street – Second Empire style, mansard roof with dormers

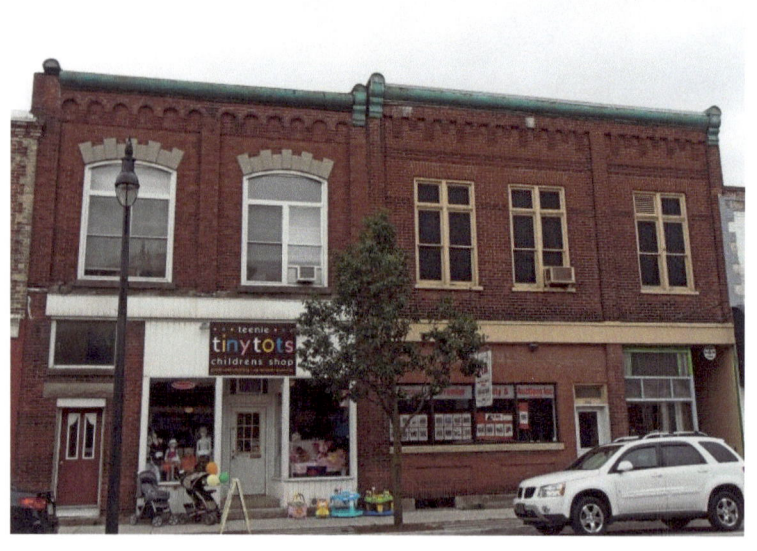

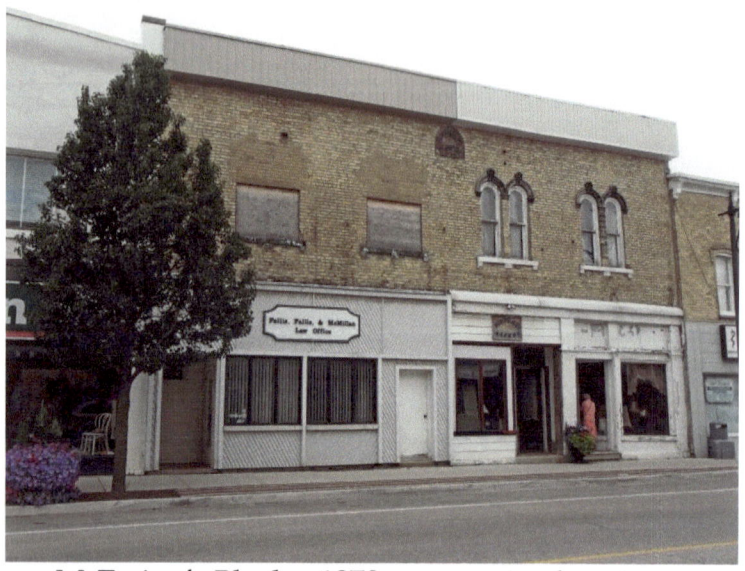

McEwing's Block – 1879 – voussoirs, keystones

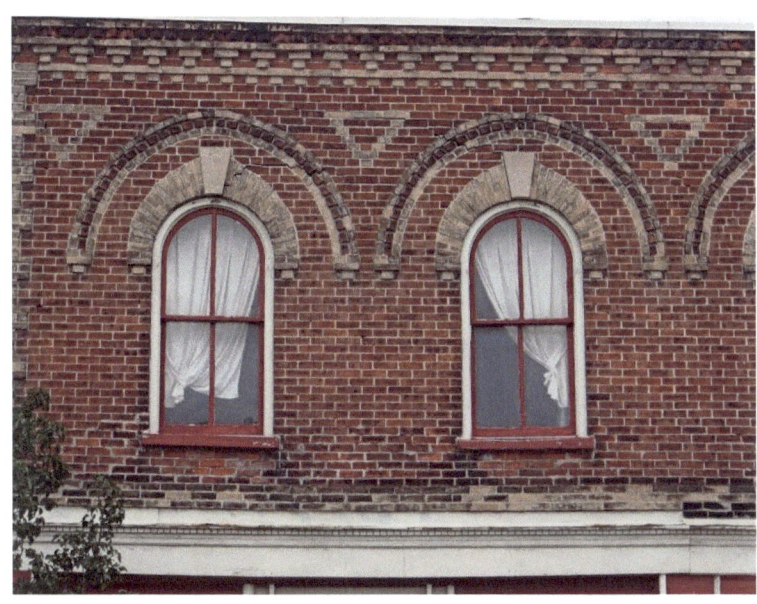

Dentil moulding, dichromatic brickwork

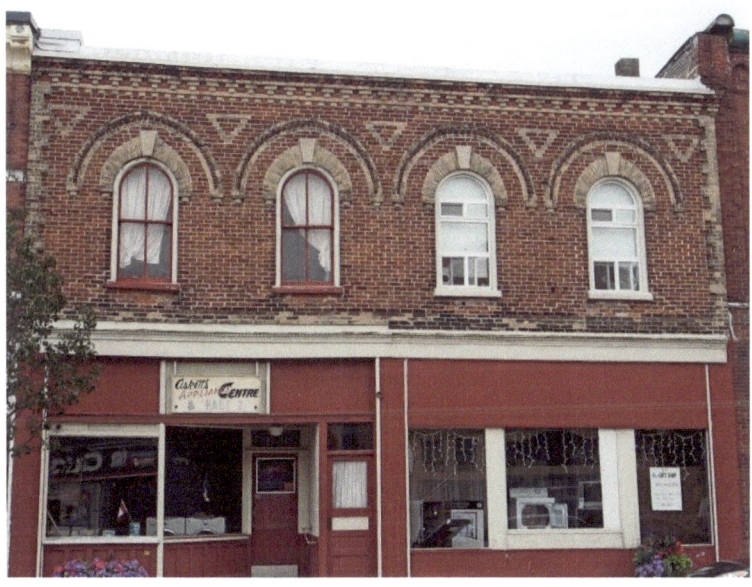

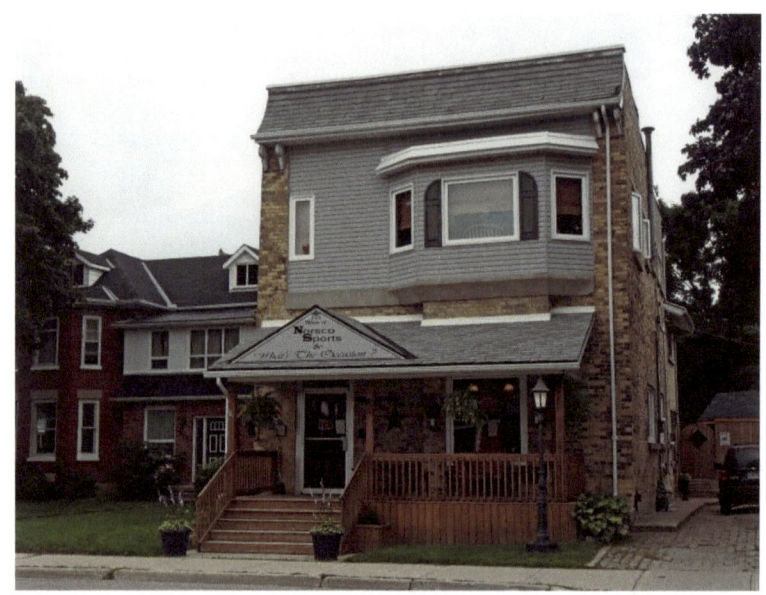

295 Main Street

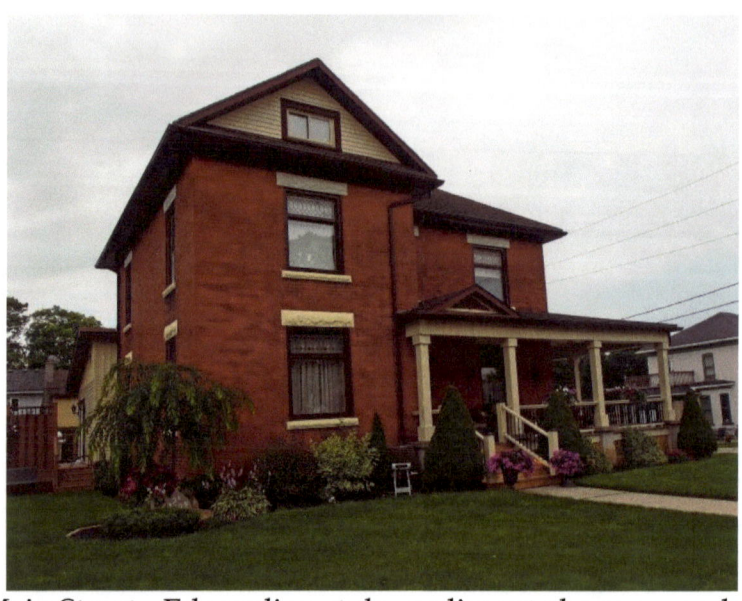

Main Street - Edwardian style, pediment above verandah

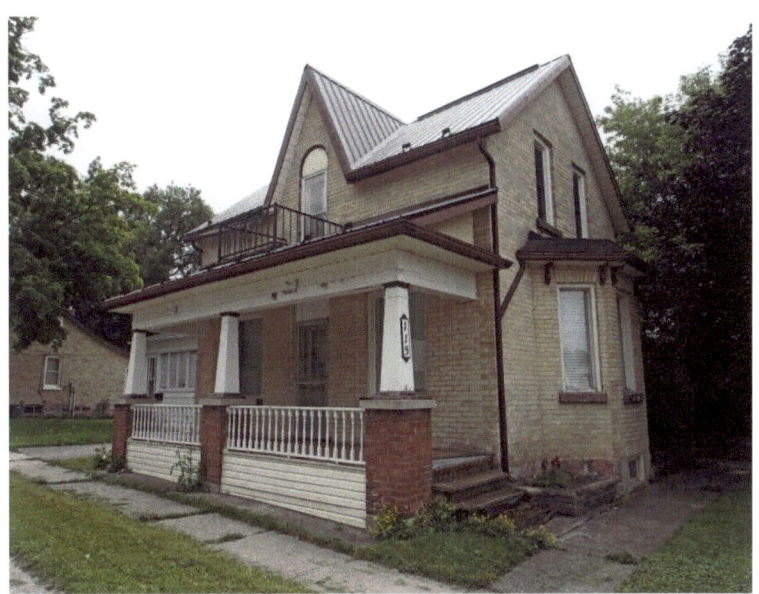

115 Minnie Street – Gothic Revival, bay window on side,
balcony above verandah

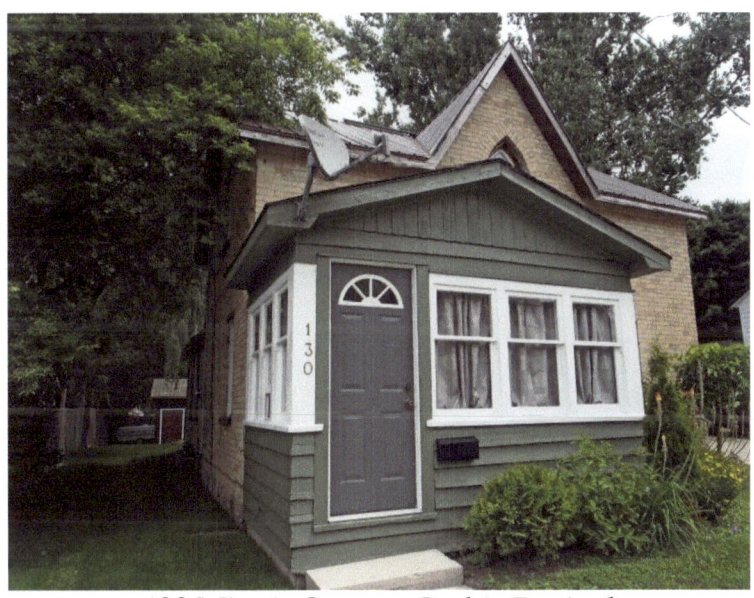

130 Minnie Street – Gothic Revival
with added enclosed front porch

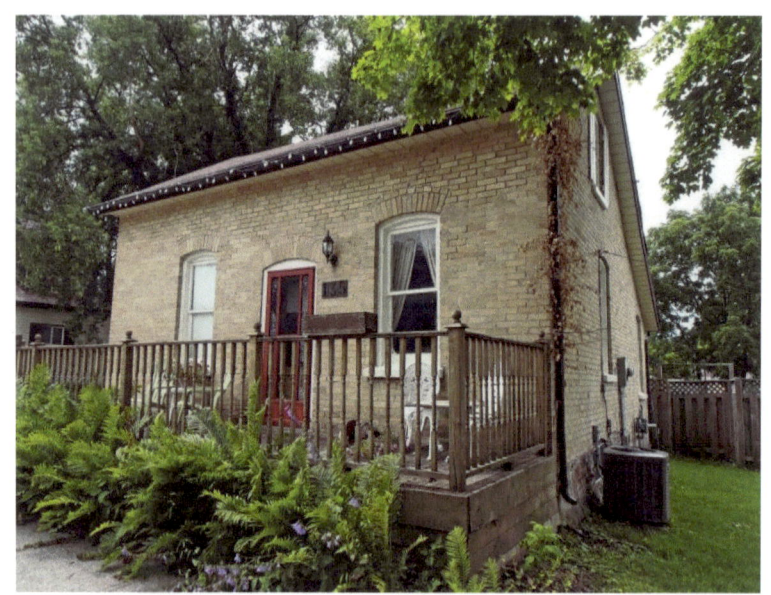

135 Minnie Street – Gothic Revival

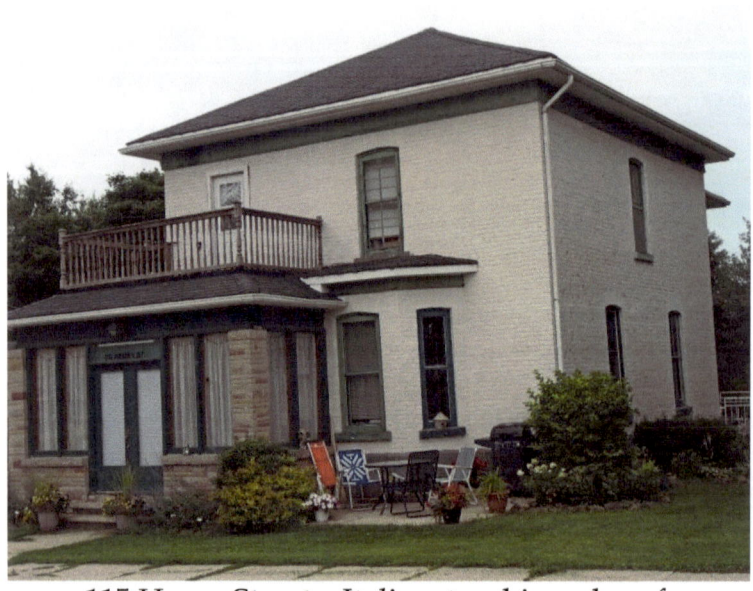

115 Henry Street – Italianate – hipped roof,
second floor balcony, ground floor bay window

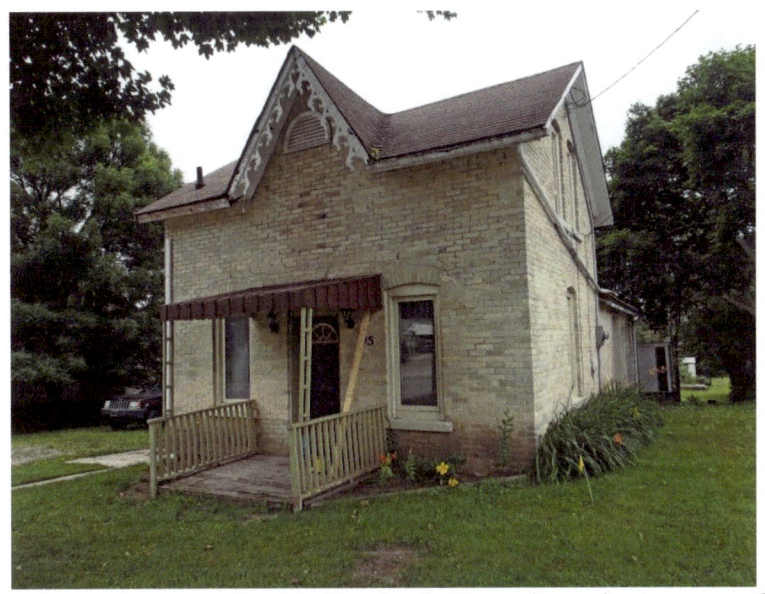

135 Henry Street – Gothic Revival, Vergeboard trim on gable

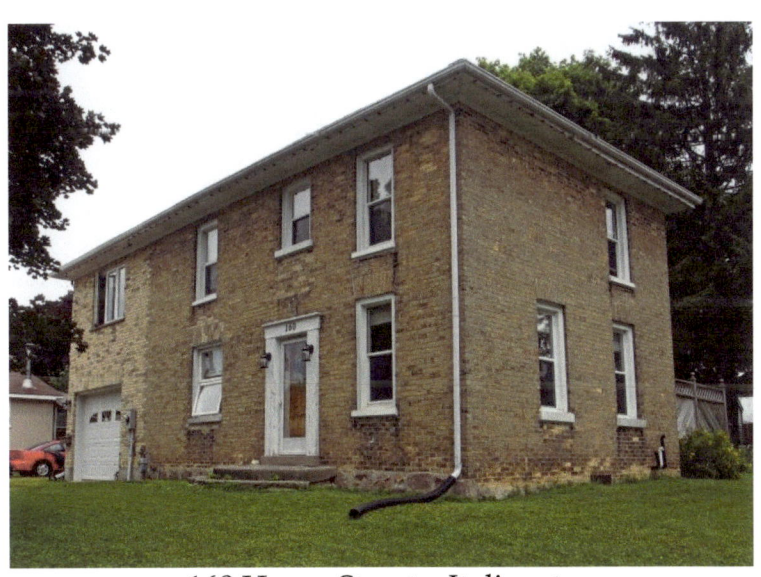

160 Henry Street – Italianate

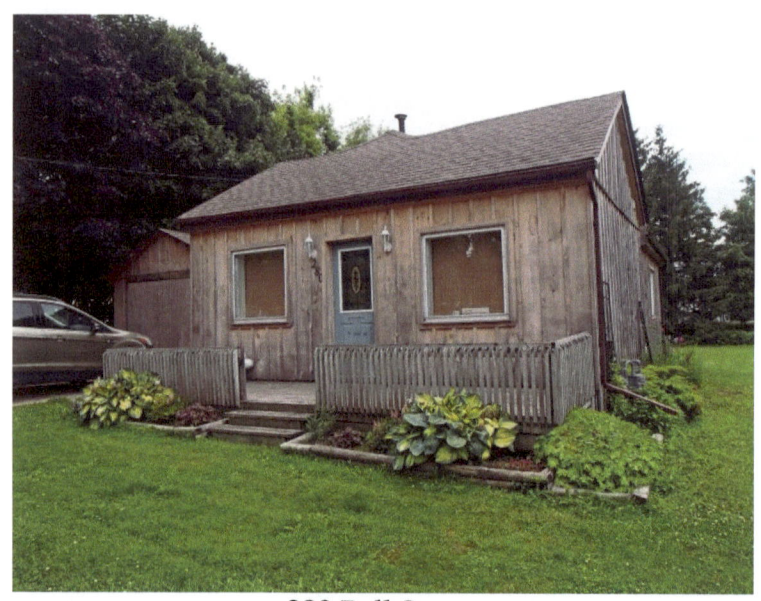

280 Bell Street

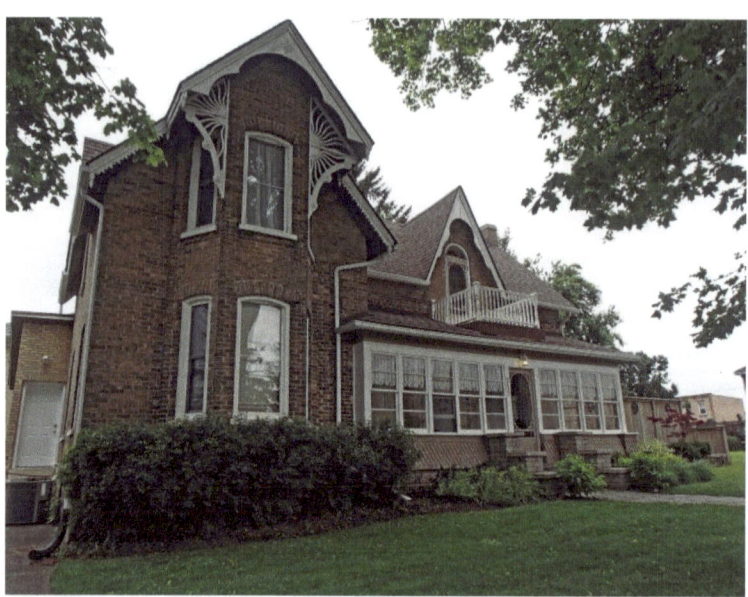

Bell Street – Gothic Revival, Vergeboard trim, fretwork

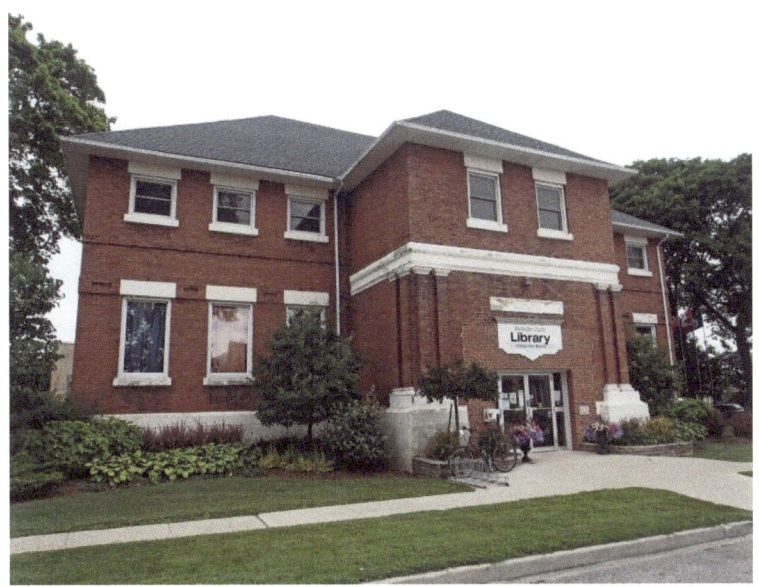

Bell Street – Library – Italianate, hipped roof

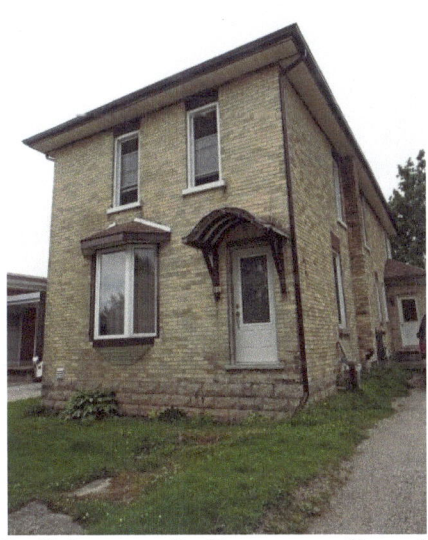

240 Bell Street – Italianate, yellow brick

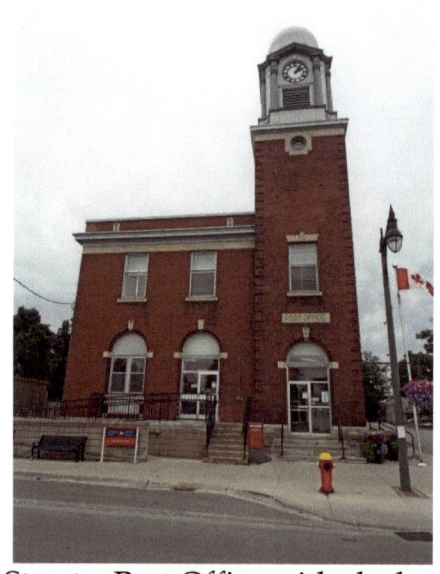

Bell Street – Post Office with clock tower

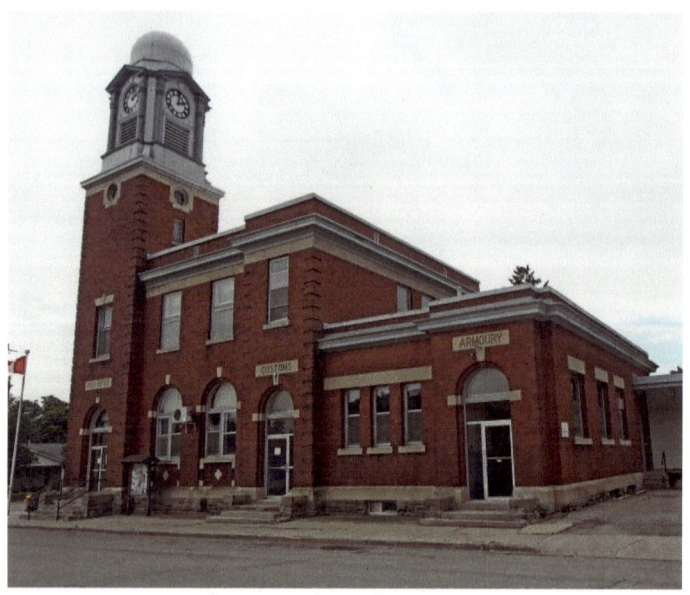

Armouries, Customs

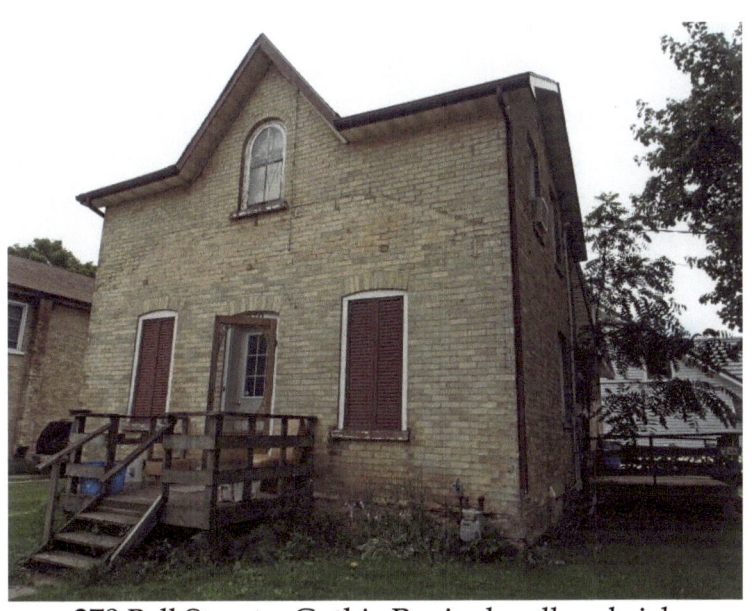

270 Bell Street – Gothic Revival, yellow brick

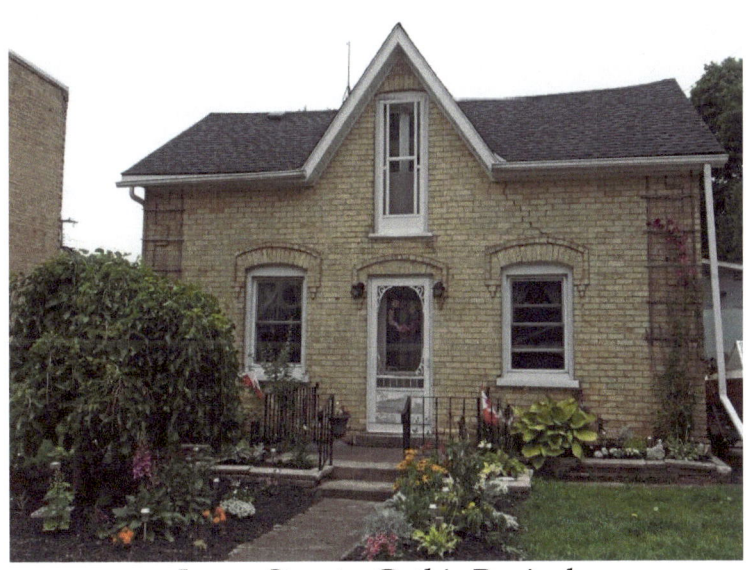

James Street – Gothic Revival

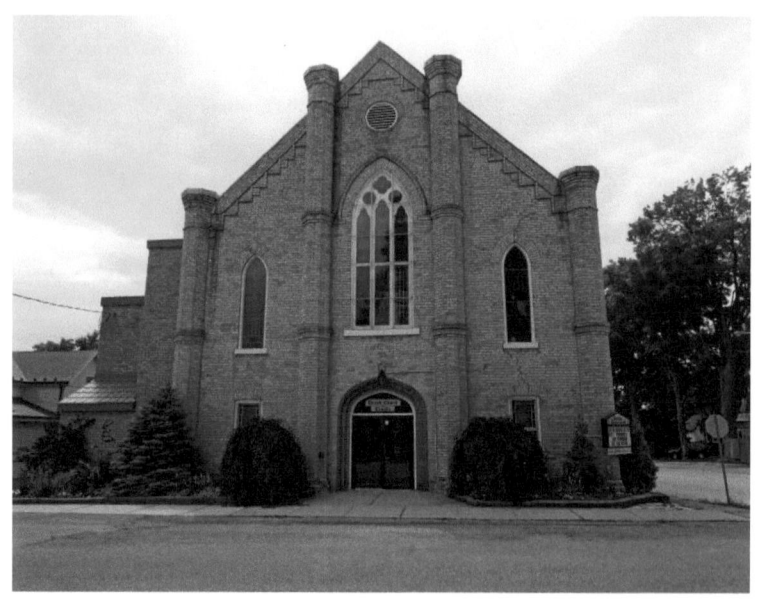

215 James Street – Palmerston United Church

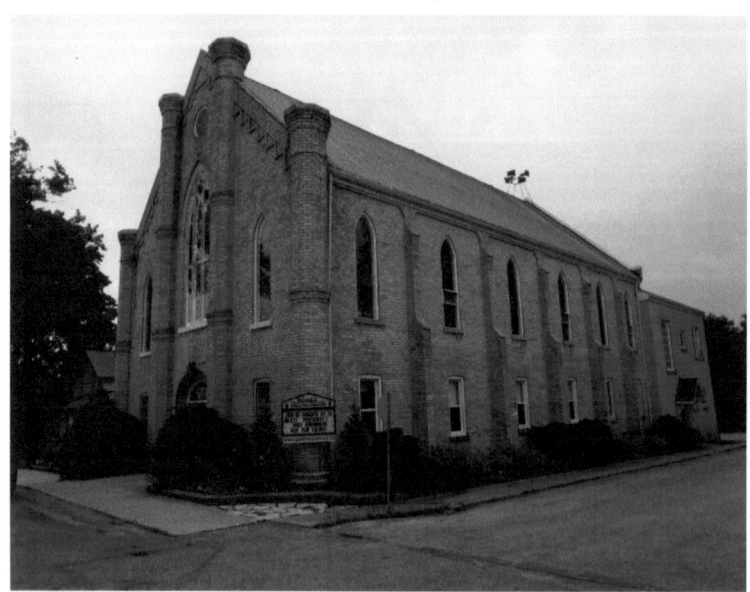

Lancet windows, buttresses

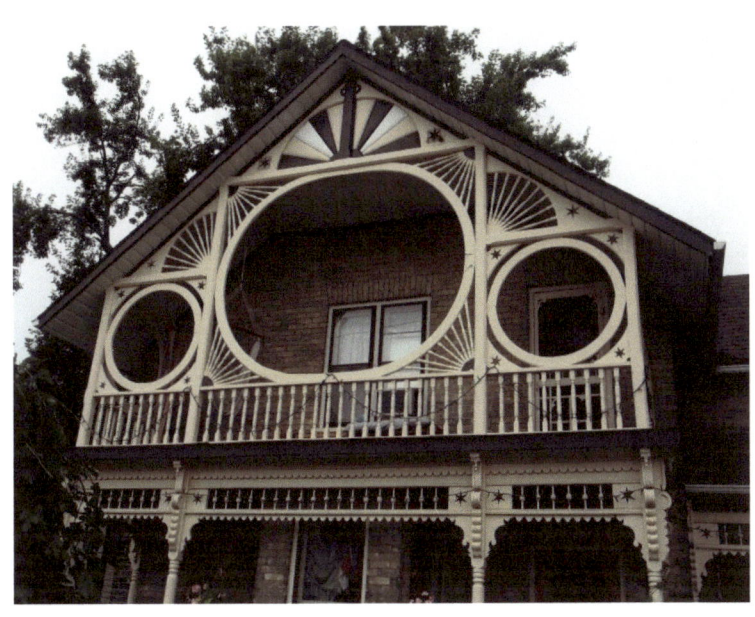

125 James Street

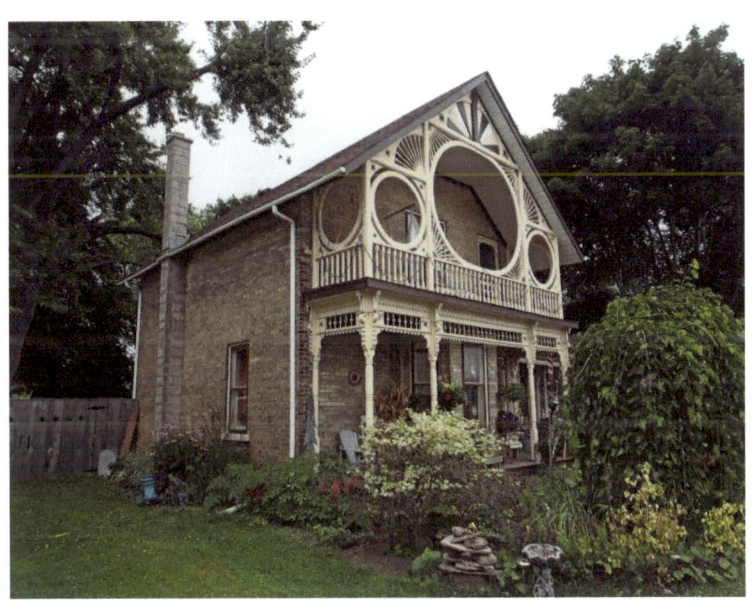

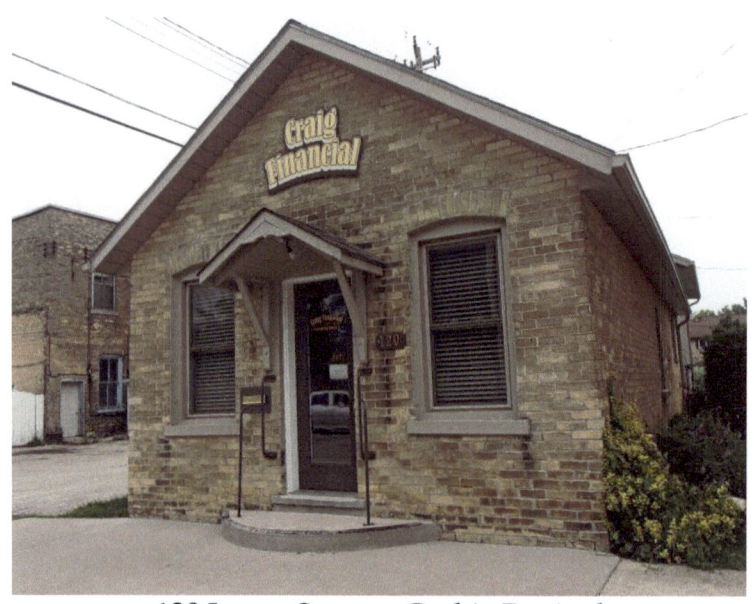

120 James Street – Gothic Revival

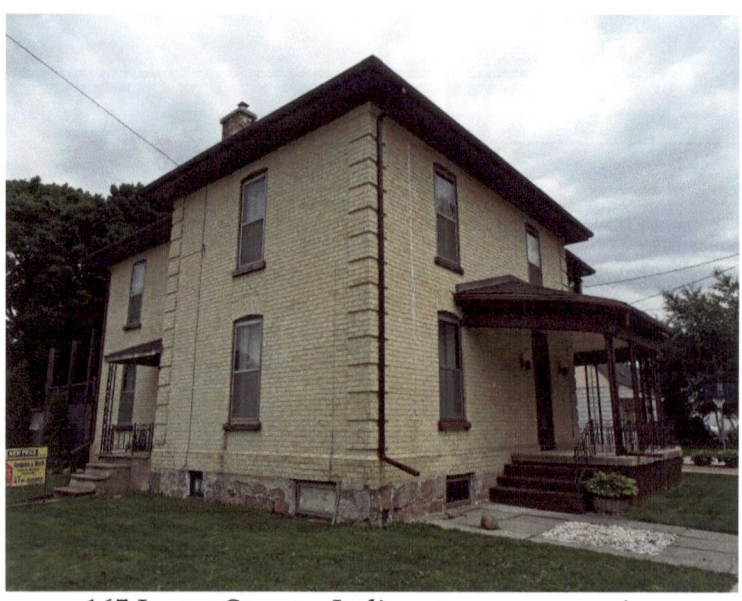

165 James Street – Italianate, corner quoins

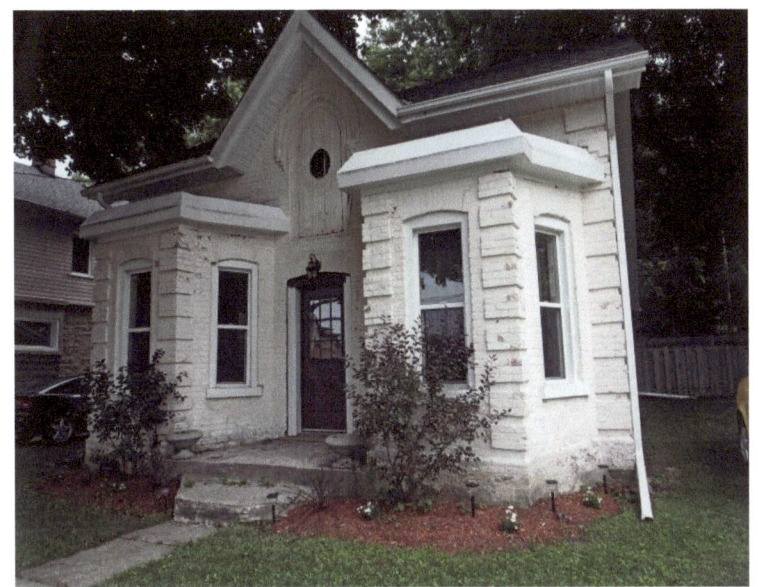

350 James Street – Gothic Revival, corner quoins,
arched door voussoir in gable

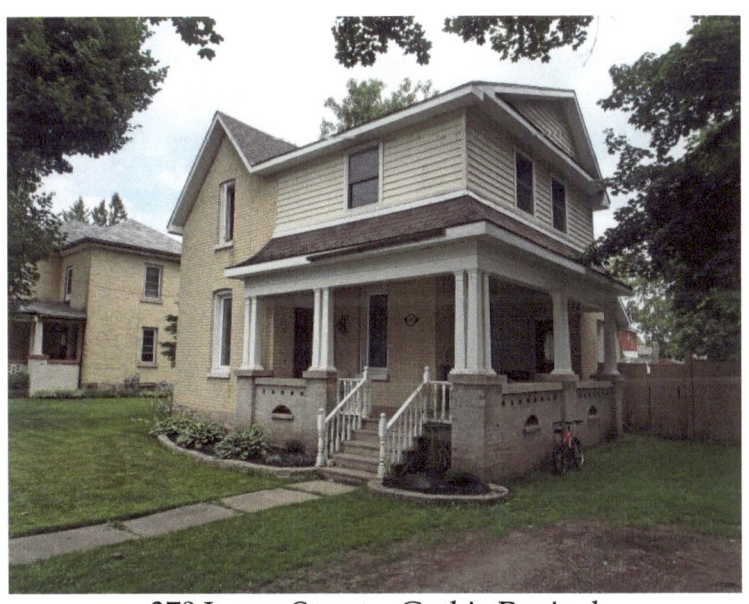

370 James Street – Gothic Revival

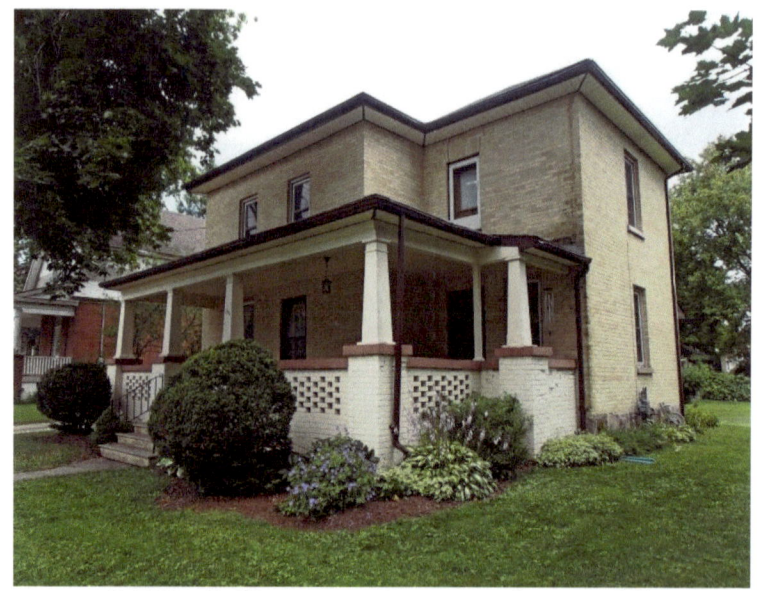

350 – Italianate, wraparound verandah

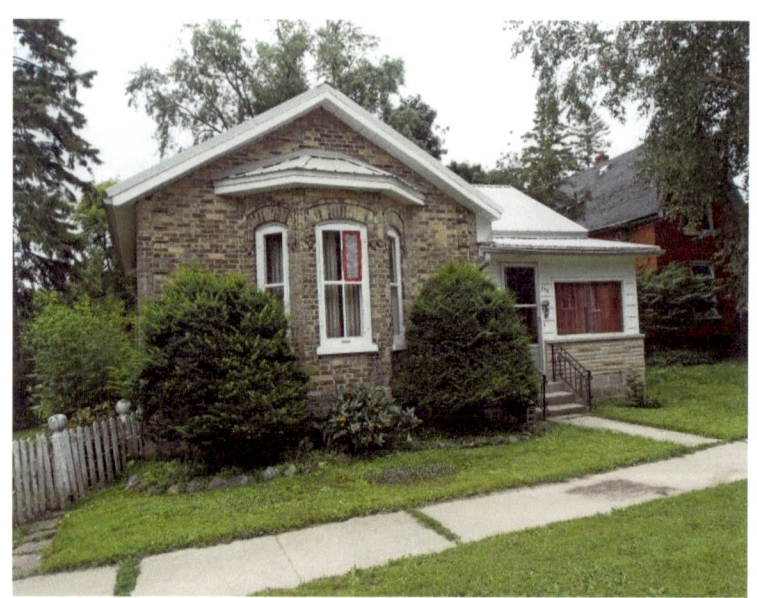

375 James Street

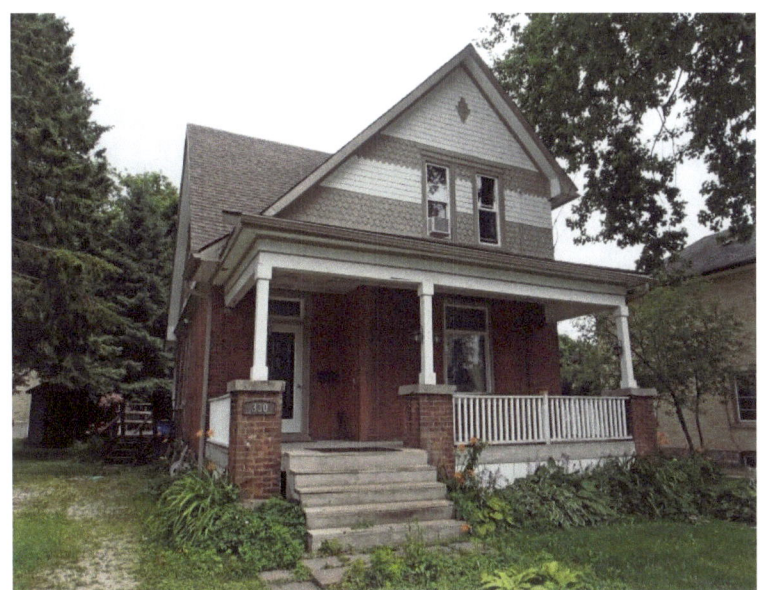

330 James Street

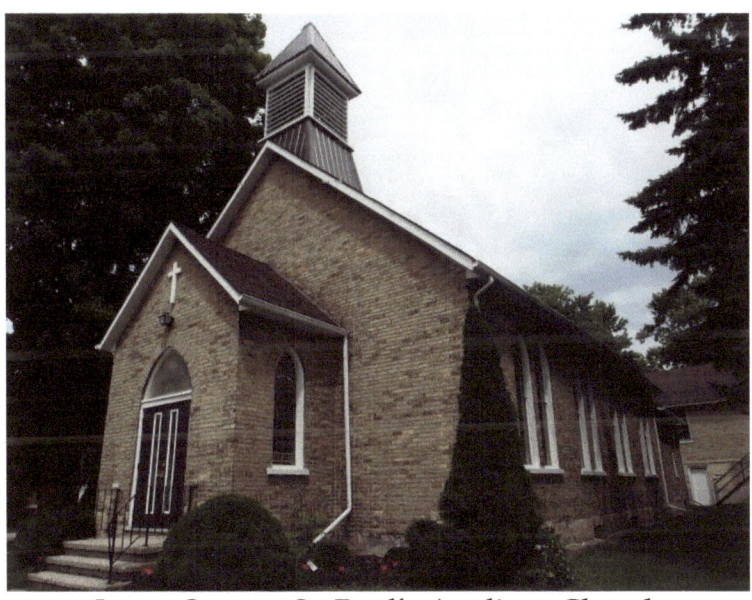

James Street – St. Paul's Anglican Church

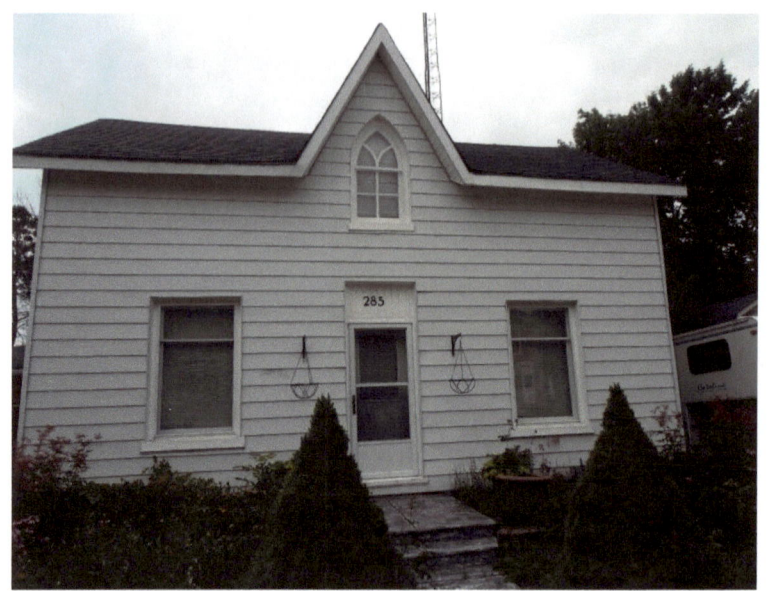

285 James Street – Gothic Revival

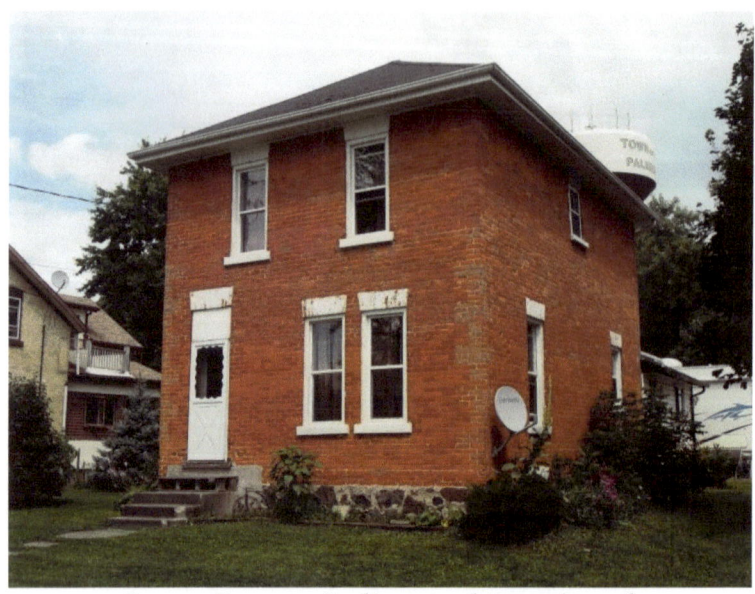

James Street – Italianate, hipped roof

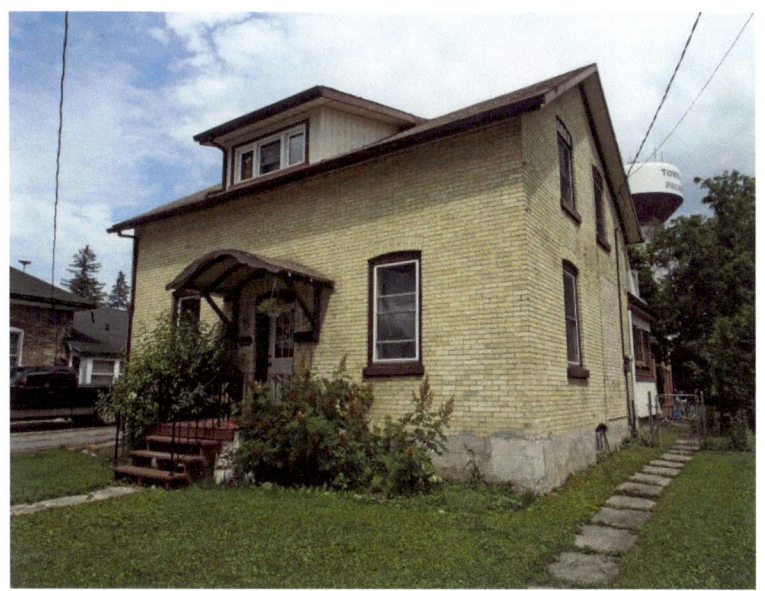

260 James Street – Gothic Revival, dormer in attic

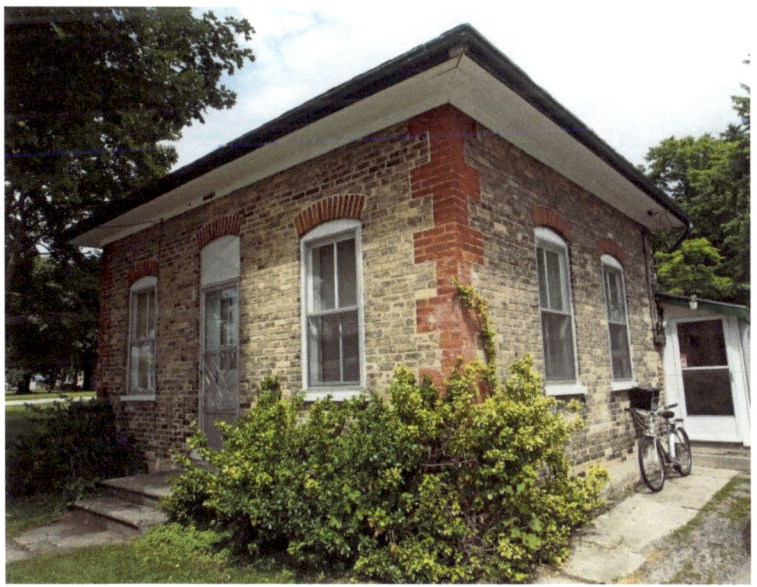

250 James Street – dichromatic brickwork, corner quoins

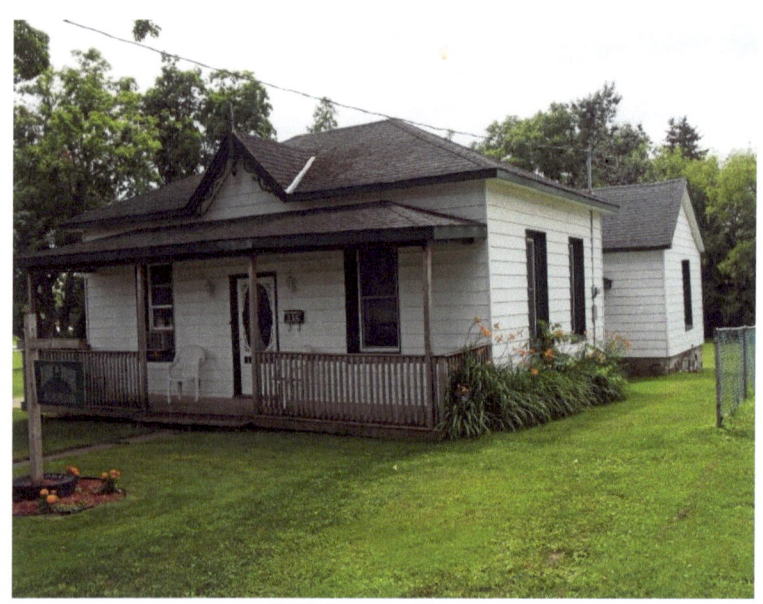

235 James Street

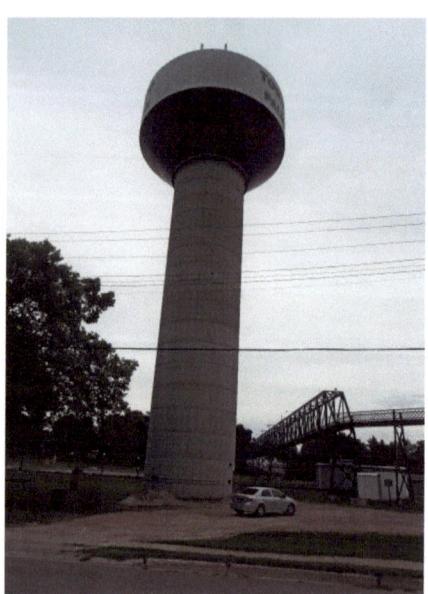

Water Tower

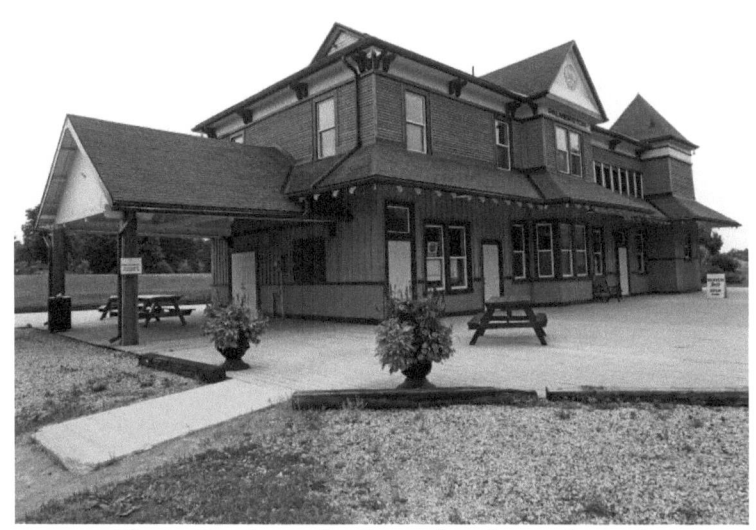

Train Station – built on land purchased
from Thomas McDowell the first settler

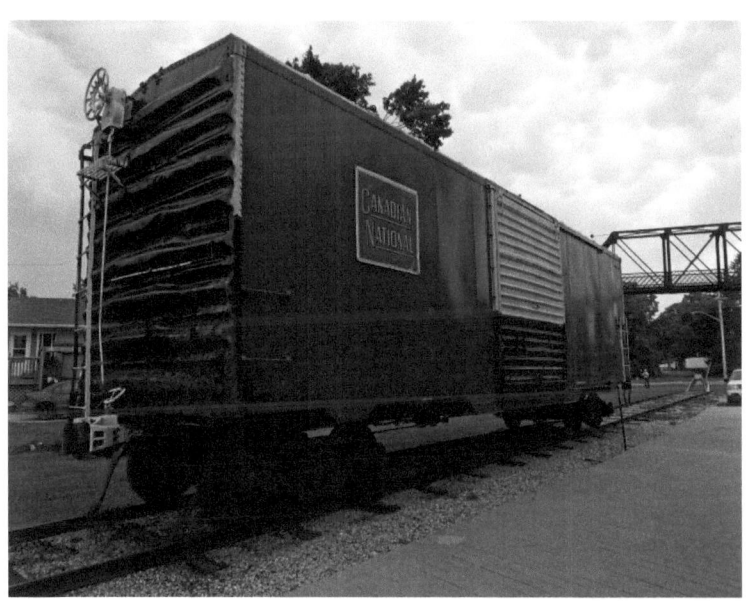

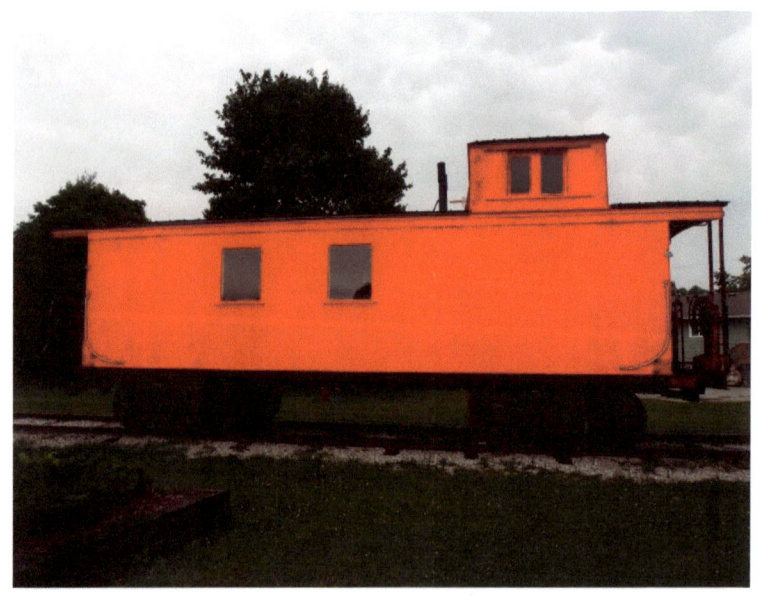

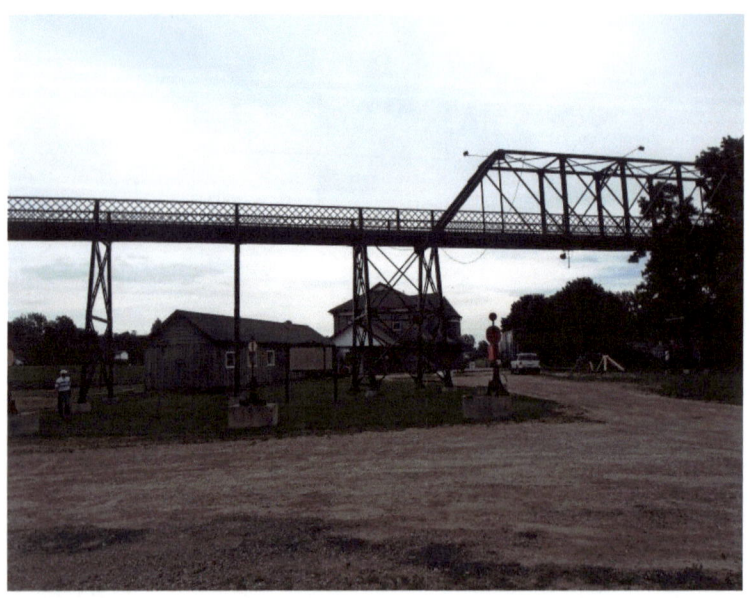

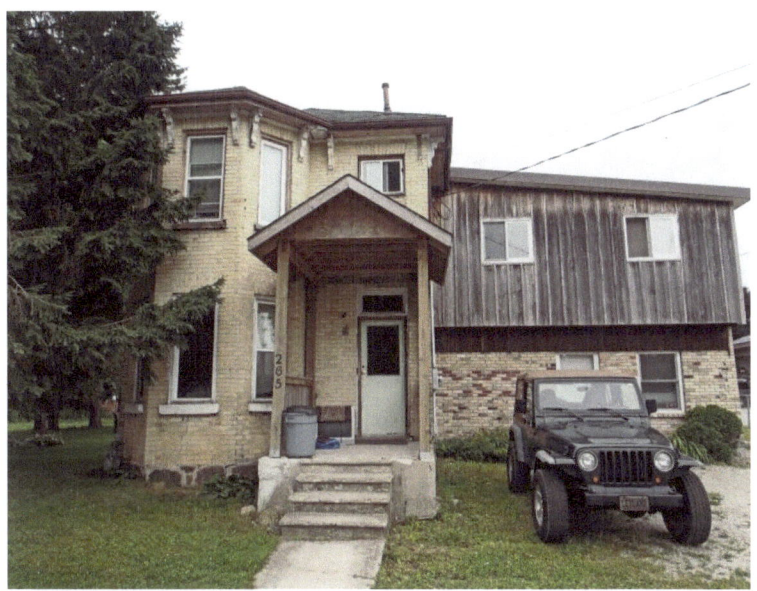

265 William Street – Italianate, cornice brackets

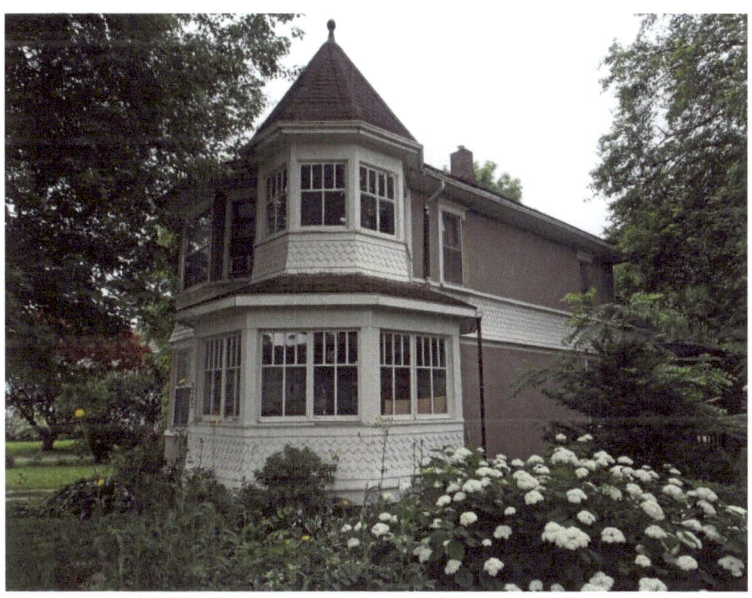

325 William Street - Queen Anne style, turret

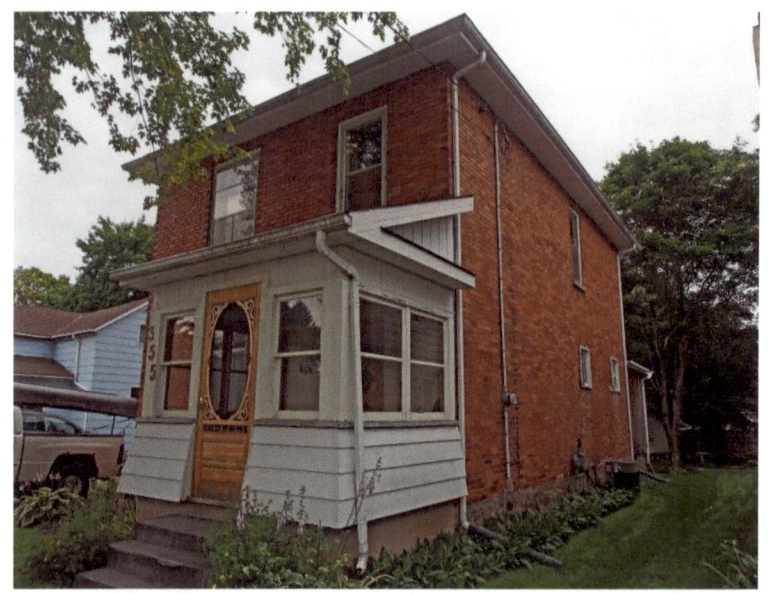

355 William Street – Italianate, hipped roof

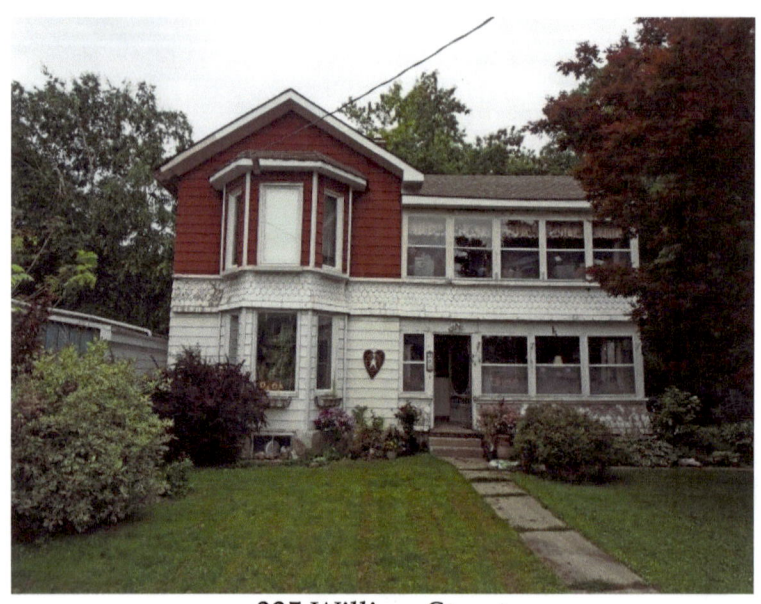

335 William Street

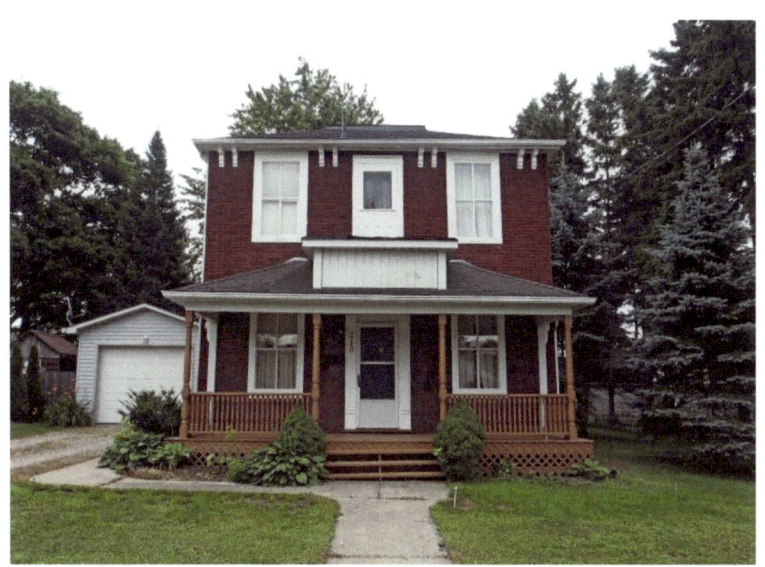

210 Queen Street – Italianate, cornice brackets

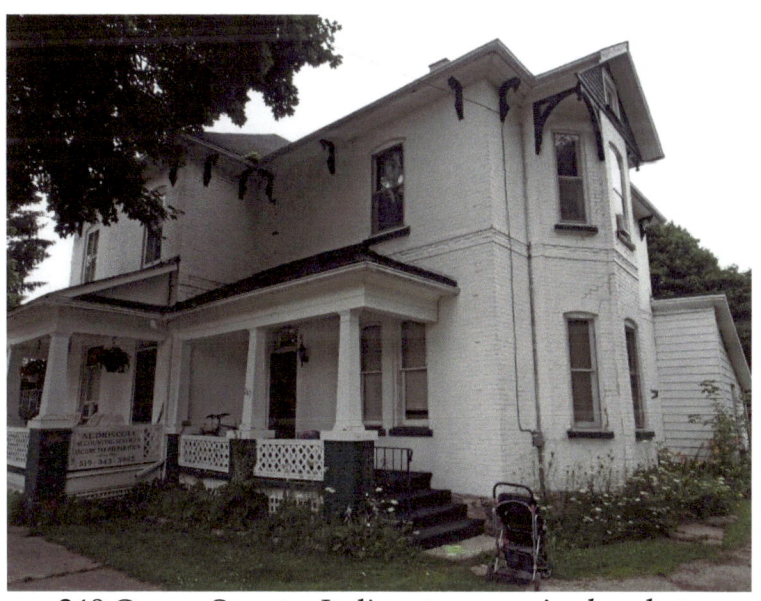

240 Queen Street – Italianate – cornice brackets

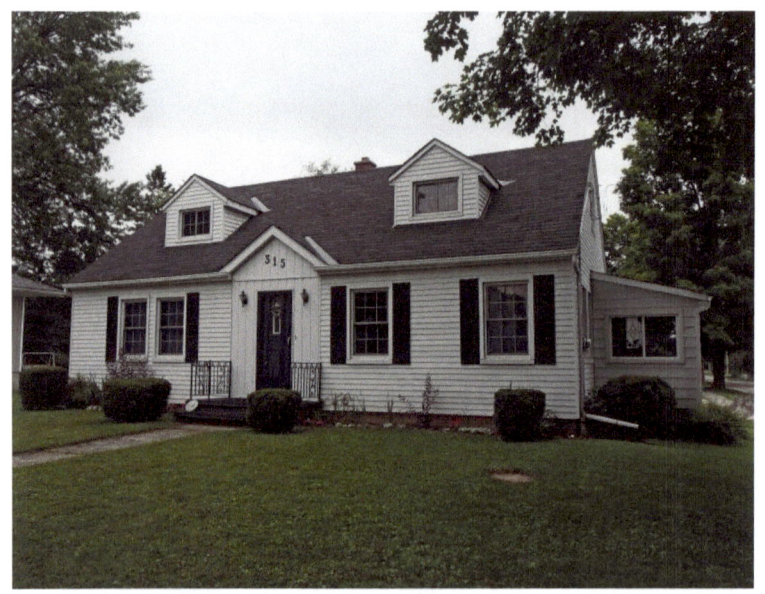

315 Queen Street – dormers in attic

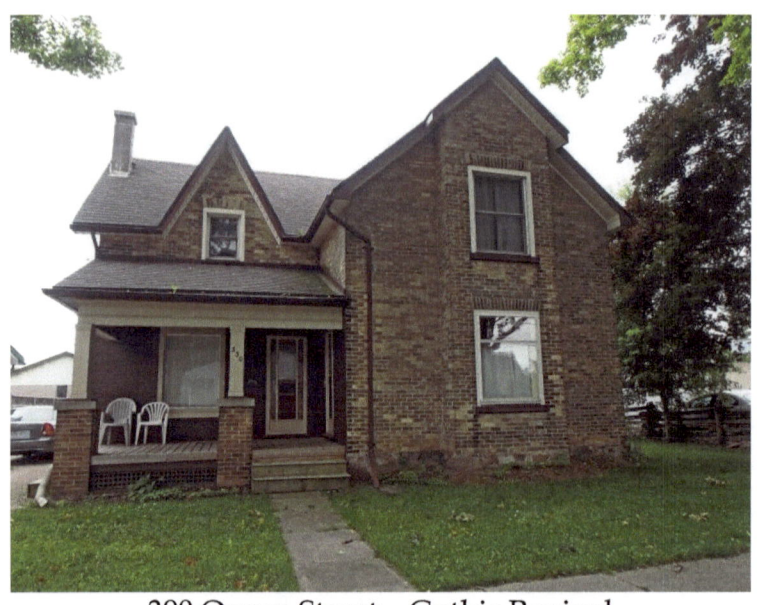

390 Queen Street – Gothic Revival

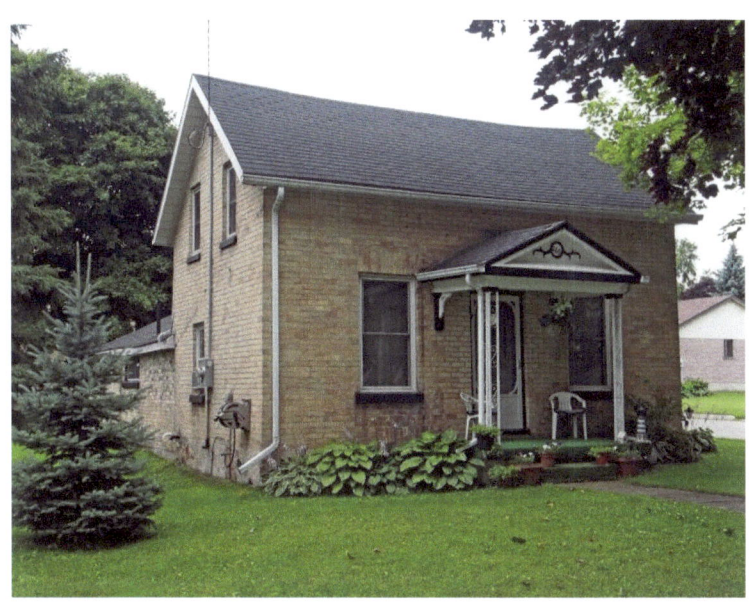

260 Queen Street – Gothic Revival, pediment above porch
with decorated tympanum

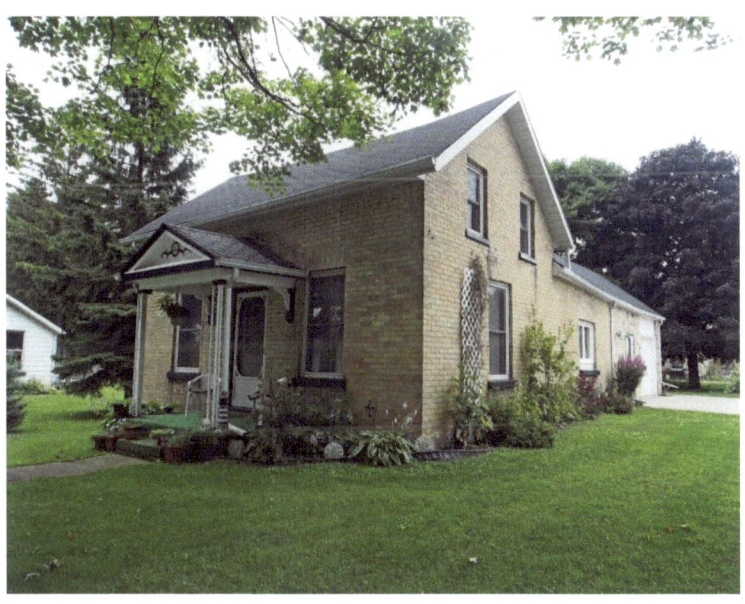

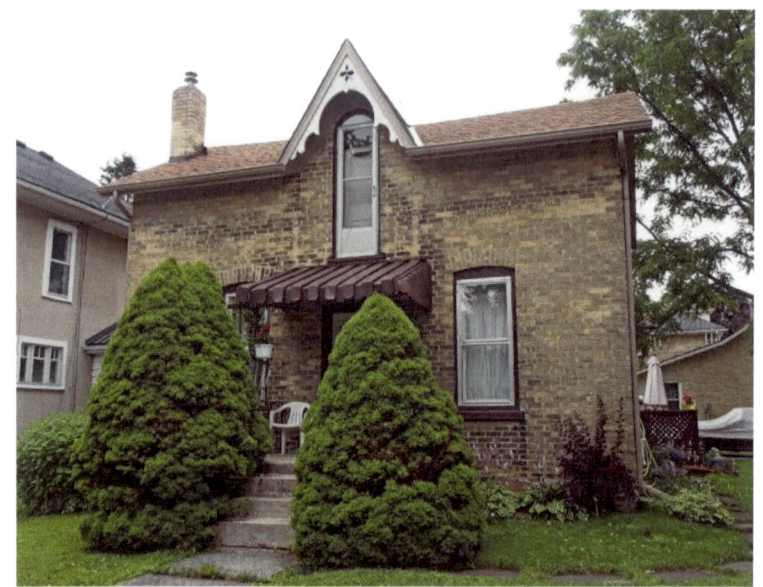

Queen Street – Gothic Revival, Vergeboard trim on gable

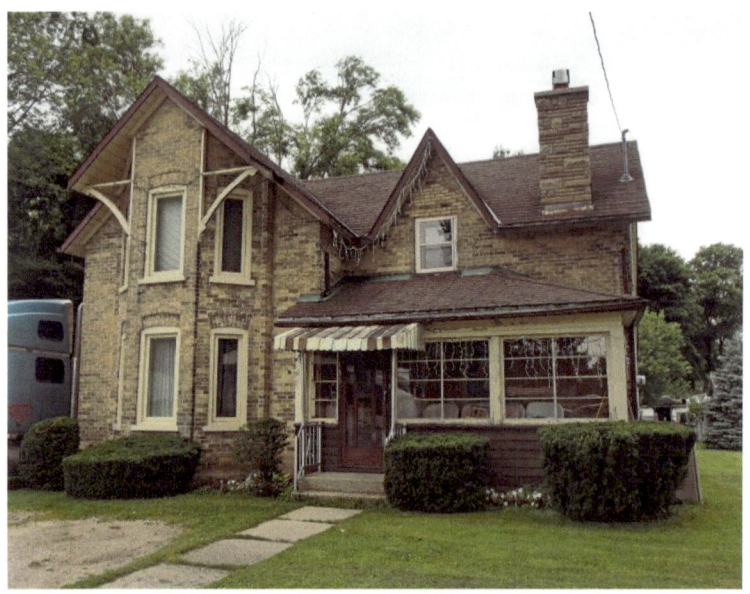

435 Queen Street – Gothic Revival

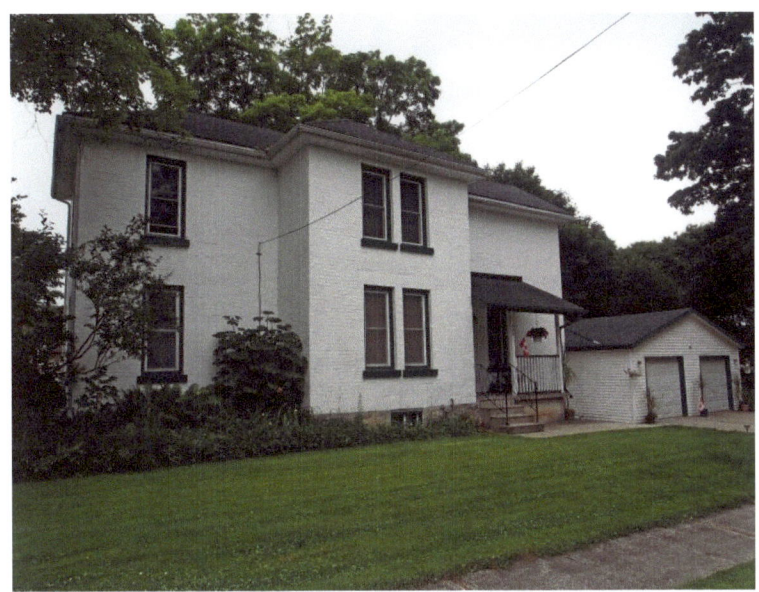

Temple Street – Italianate, hipped roof

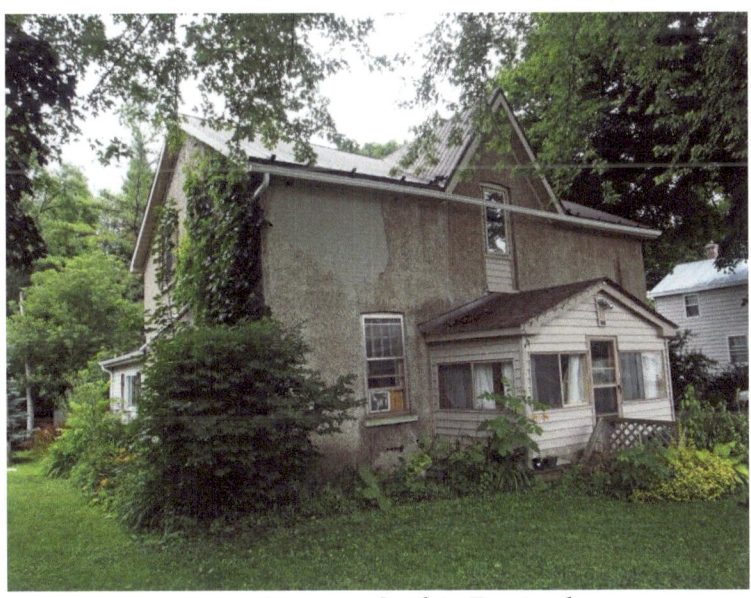

King Street – Gothic Revival

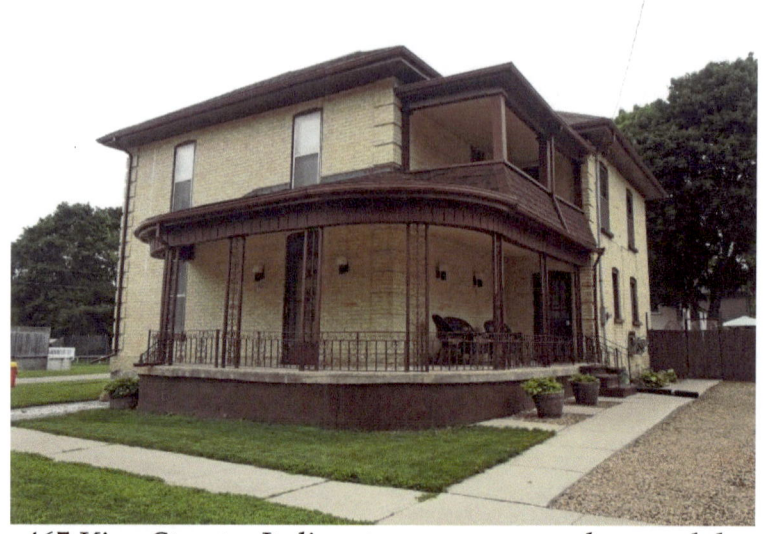

465 King Street – Italianate – wraparound verandah, second floor balcony, hipped roof, corner quoins

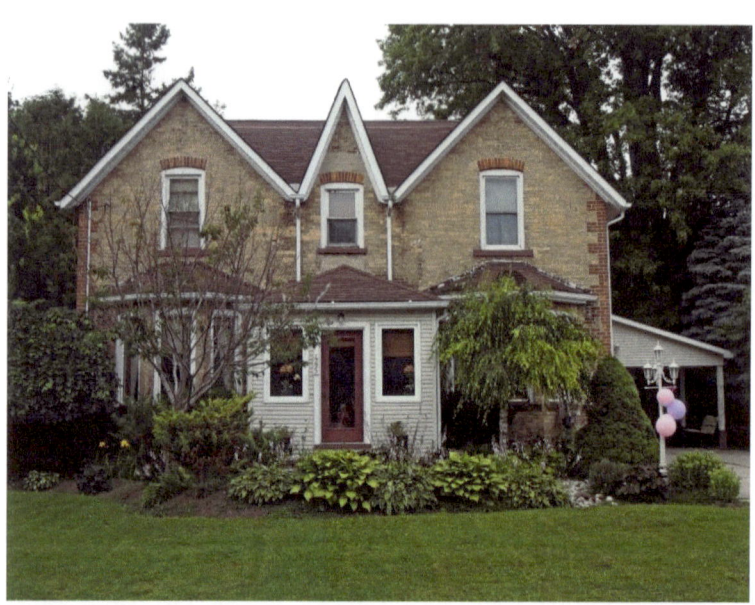

485 King Street – triple gable Gothic Revival, dichromatic brickwork, corner quoins, bay windows

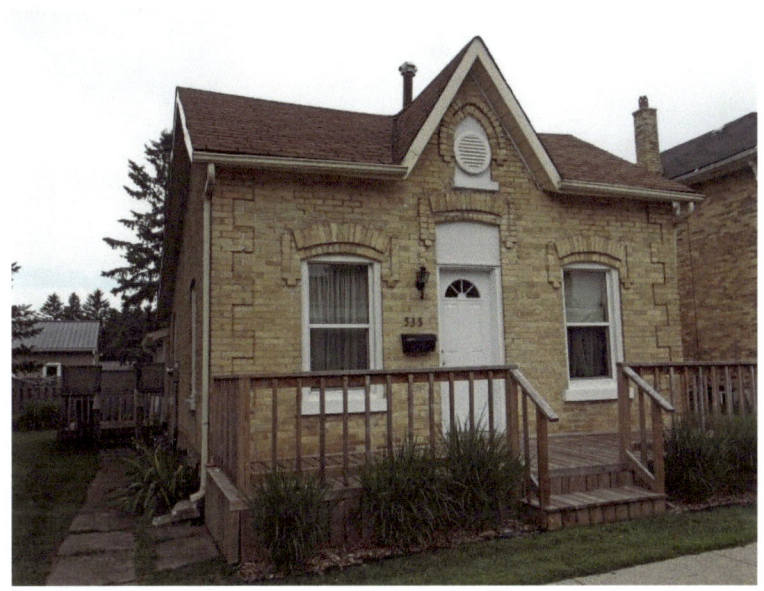

535 King Street – Gothic Revival, corner quoins, arched window voussoirs

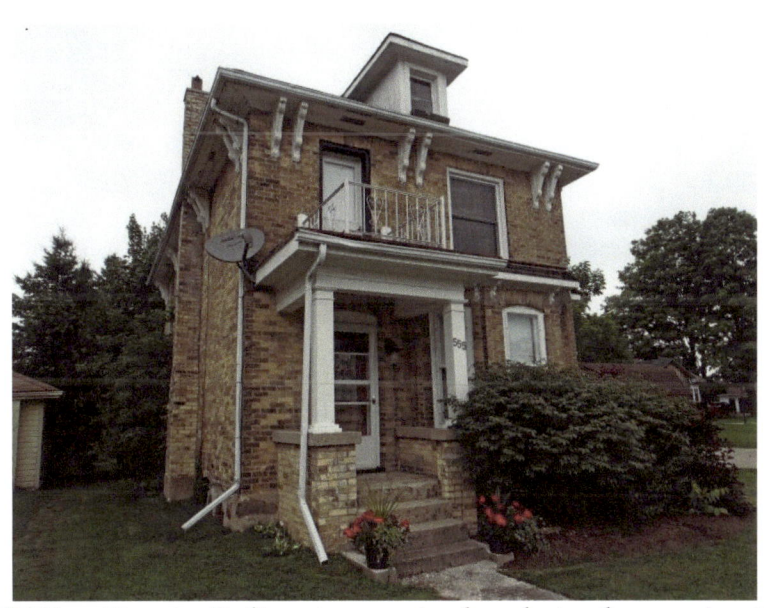

555 King Street – Italianate, cornice brackets, dormer in attic

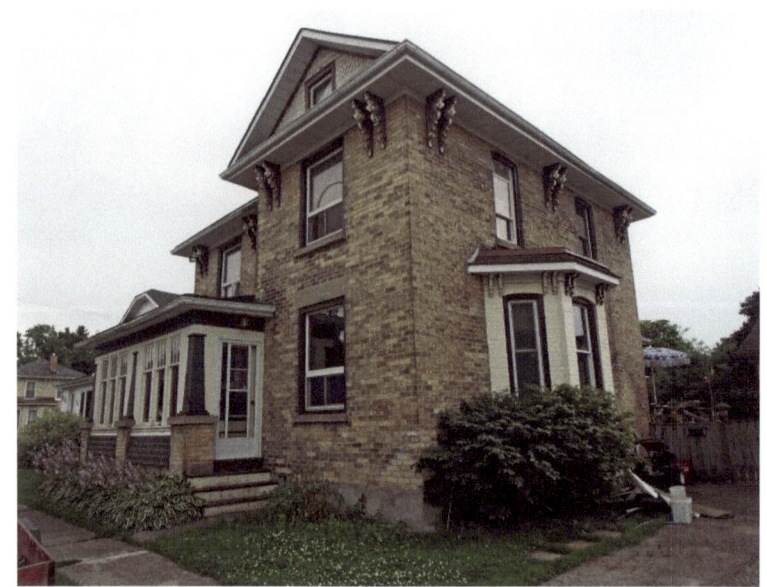

560 King Street – Italianate, cornice brackets, bay window

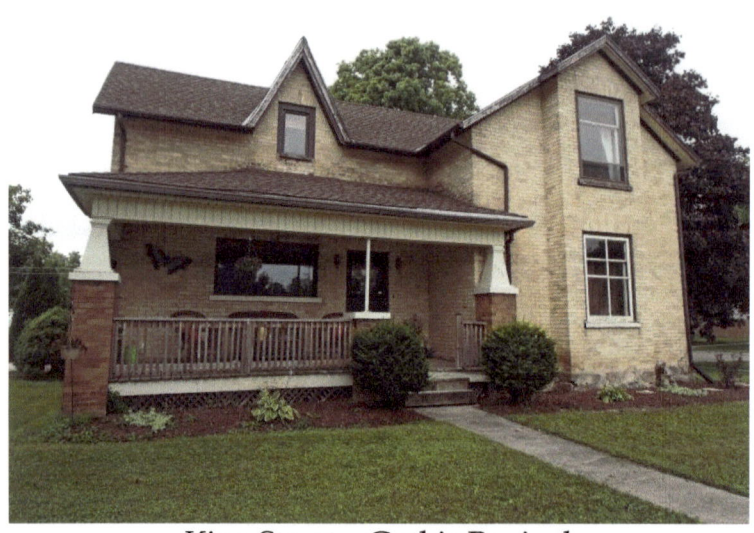

King Street – Gothic Revival

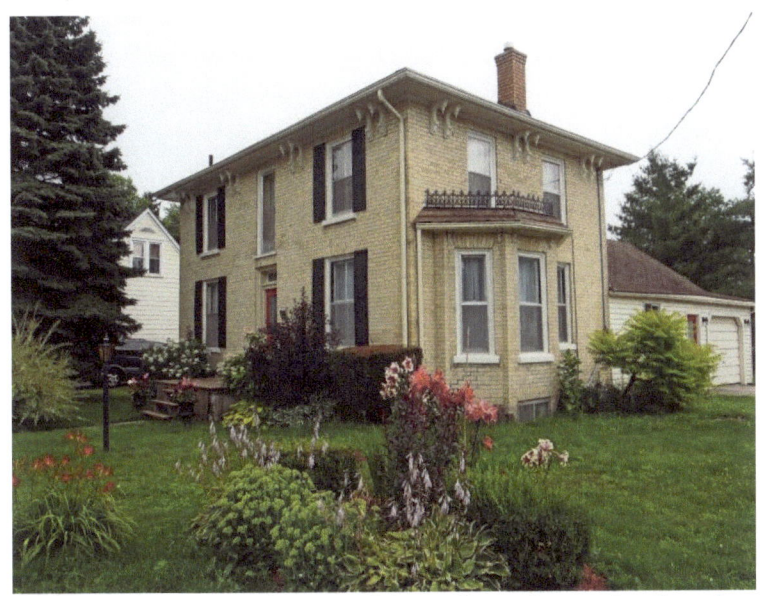

620 King Street – Italianate, hipped roof, cornice brackets,
iron cresting above bay window

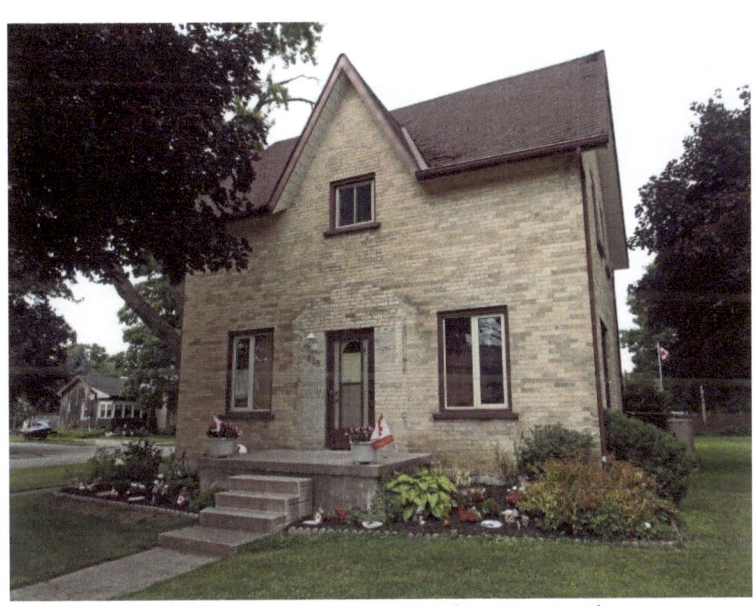

625 King Street – Gothic Revival

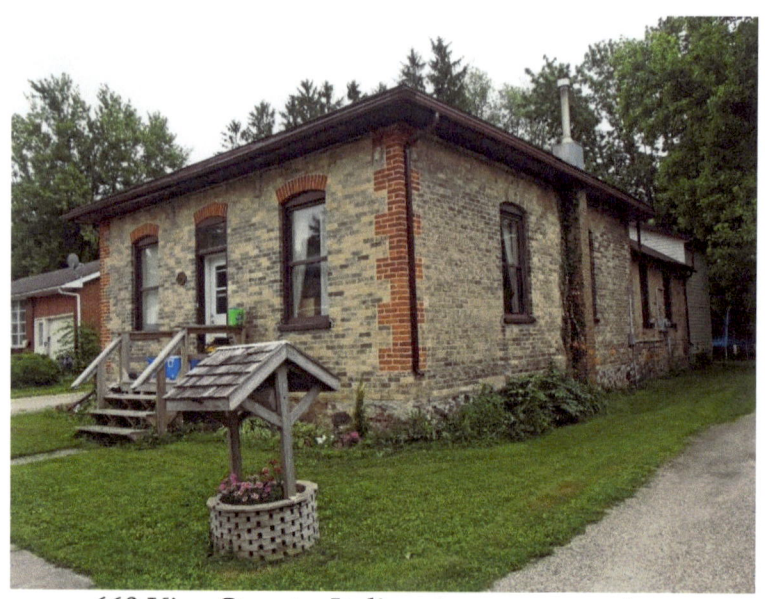

660 King Street – Italianate, corner quoins,
Dichromatic brickwork

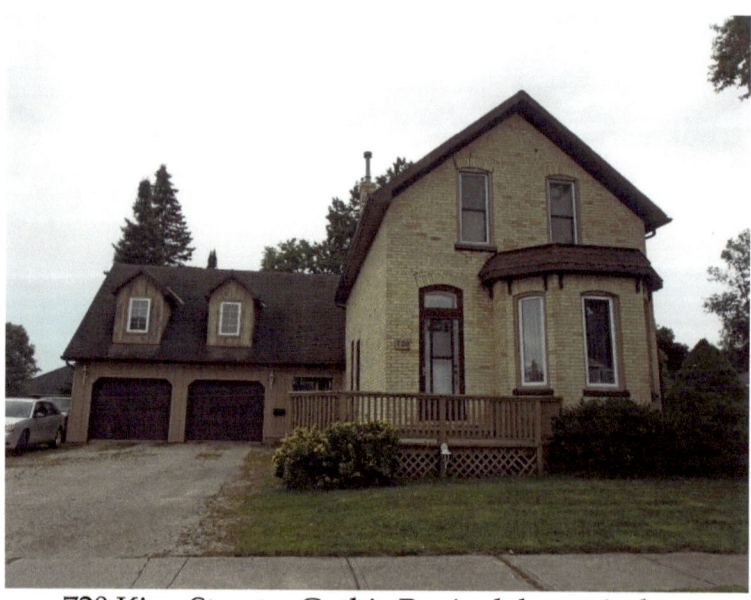

720 King Street – Gothic Revival, bay window

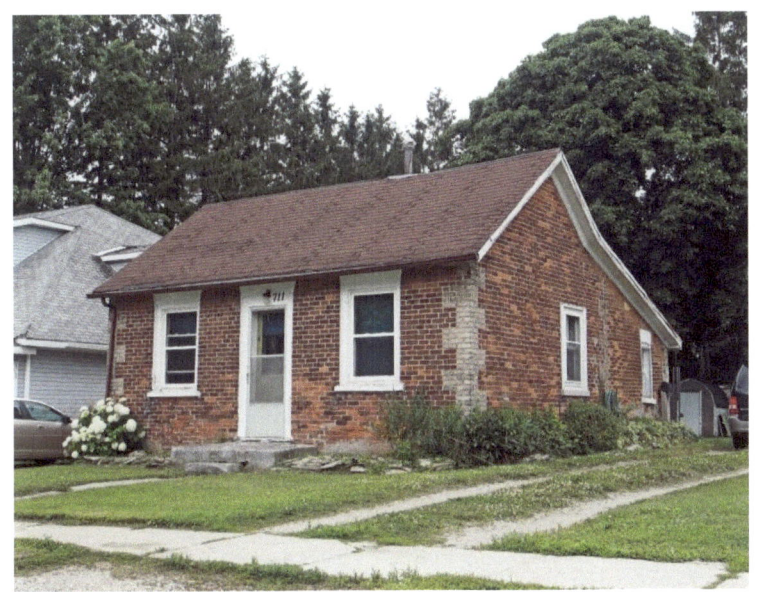

711 King Street – corner quoins

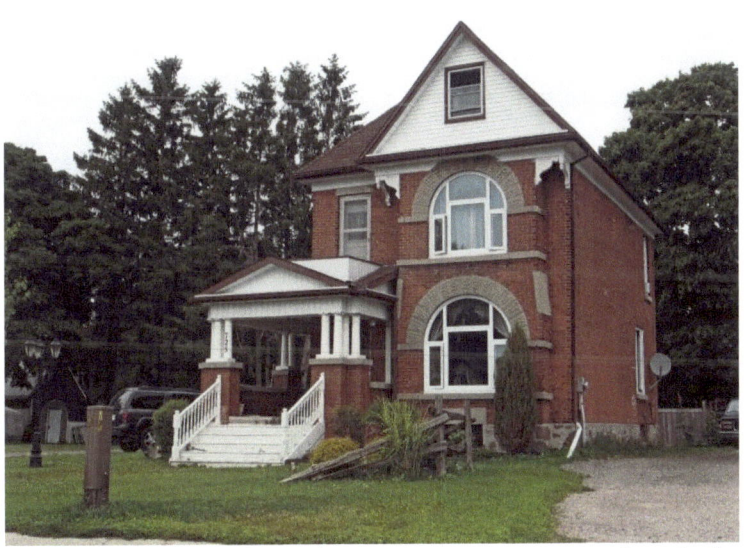

725 King Street – Edwardian – Romanesque style window
voussoirs, fretwork, pediment above verandah

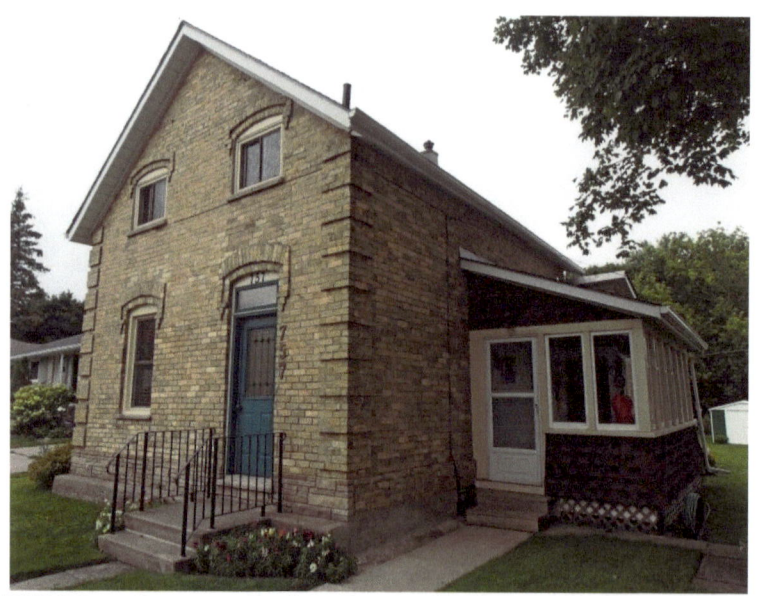

757 King Street – Gothic Revival, corner quoins, arched window voussoirs

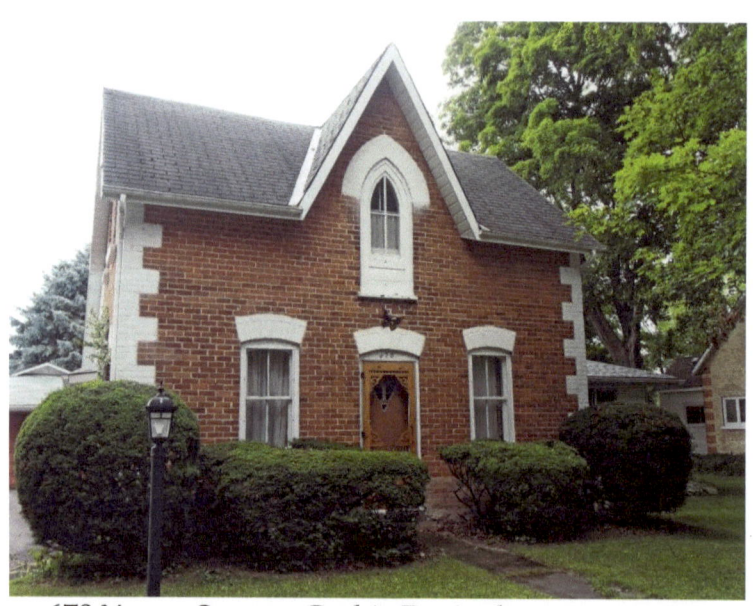

670 Yonge Street – Gothic Revival, corner quoins

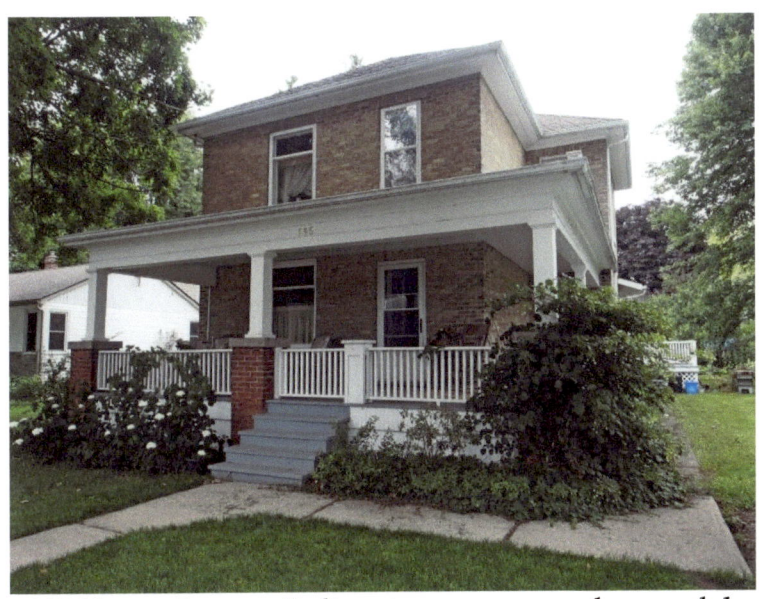

665 Yonge Street – Italianate, wraparound verandah

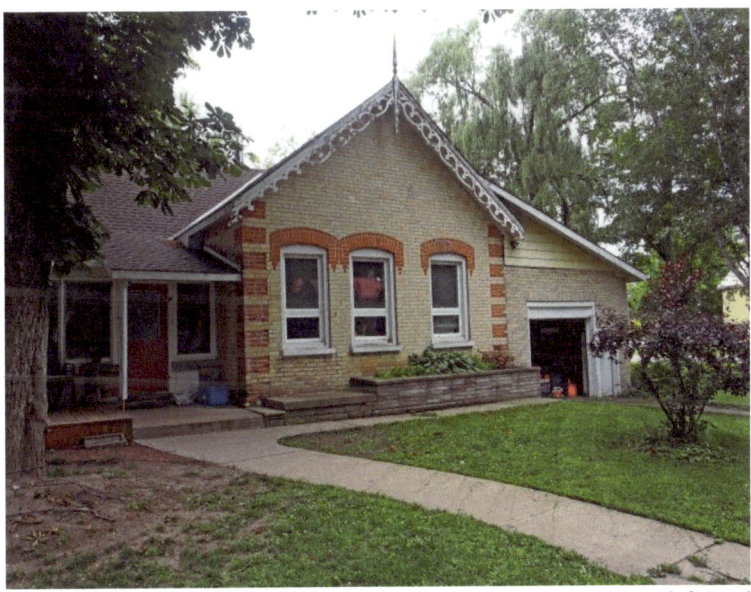

Yonge Street – Gothic Revival, Vergeboard trim and finial on
gable, dichromatic brickwork, corner quoins

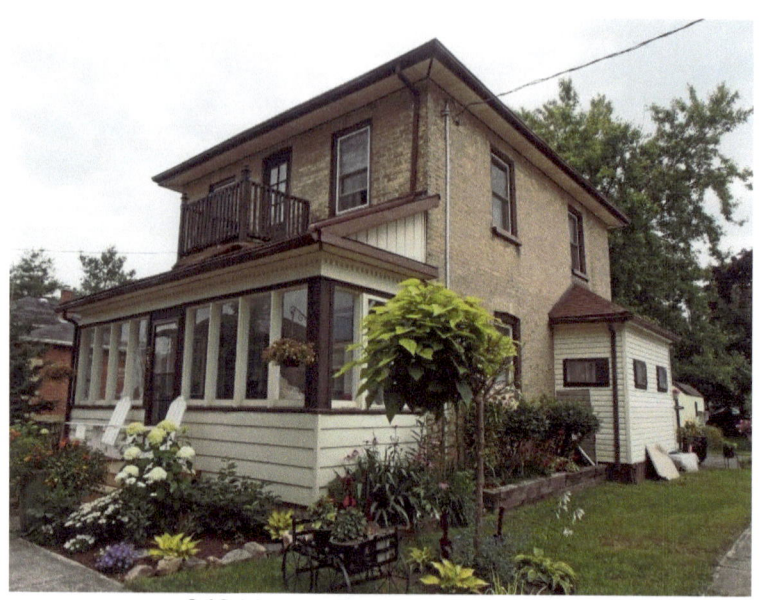

360 Yonge Street – Italianate

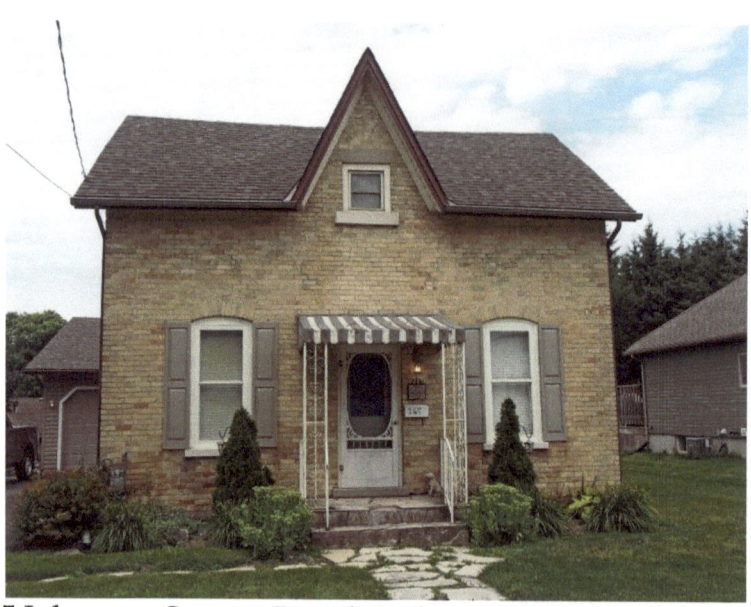

265 Inkerman Street – David Zurbrigg, Photographer - 1902

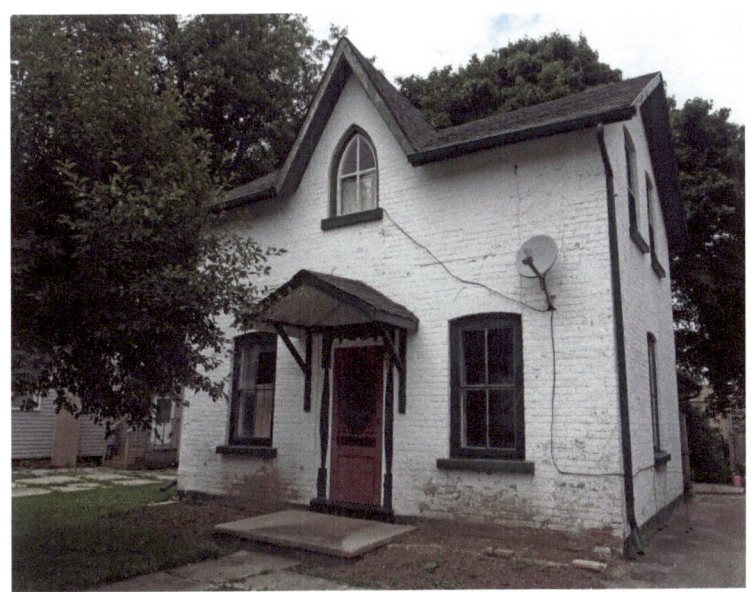

Inkerman Street – Gothic Revival

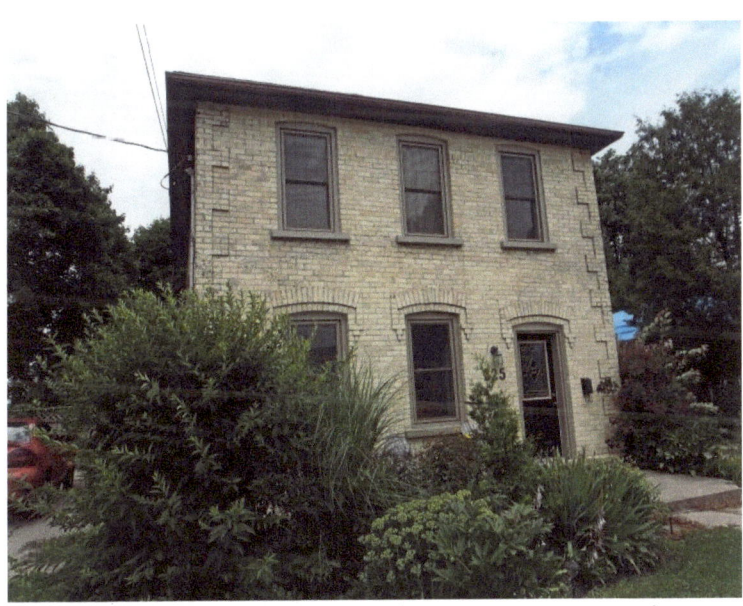

225 Inkerman Street – Italianate, corner quoins

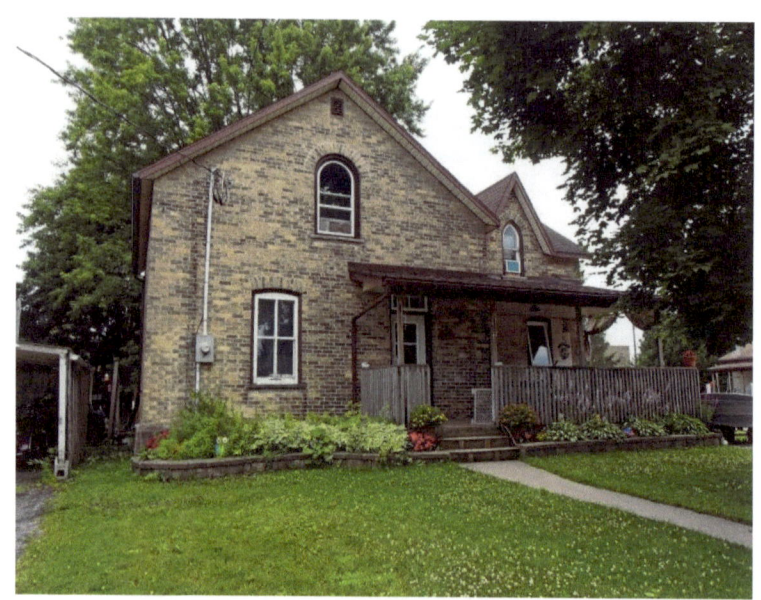

220 Inkerman Street – Gothic Revival

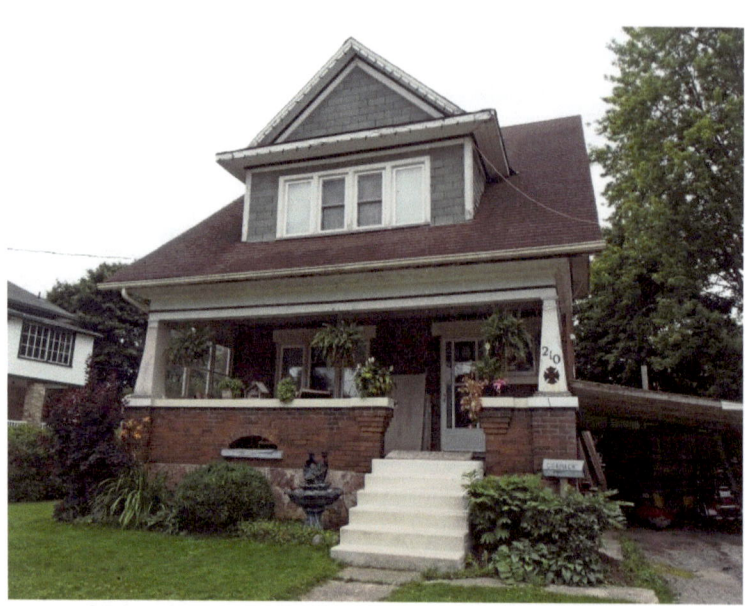

210 Inkerman Street – large dormer in attic

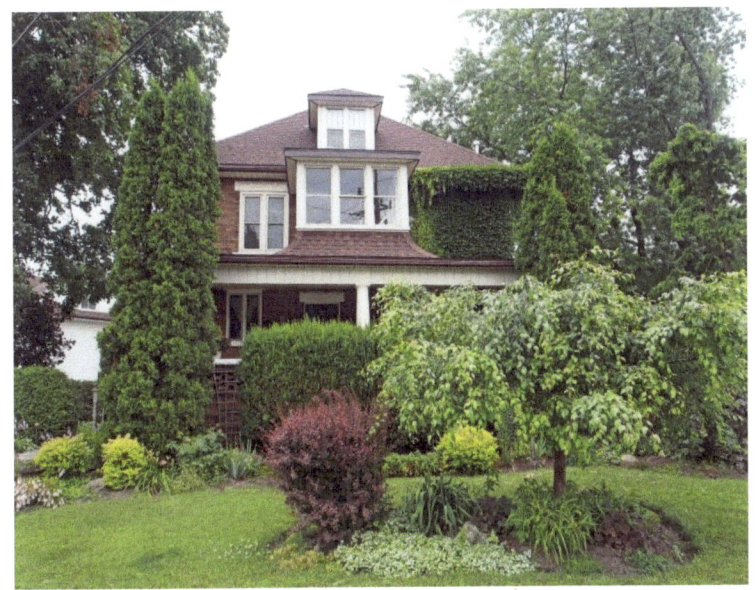

Jane Street

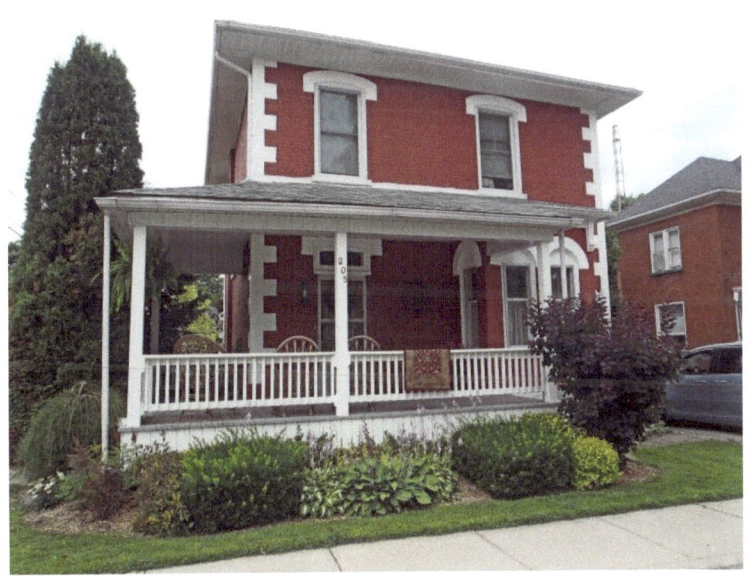

205 Jane Street – Italianate, corner quoins

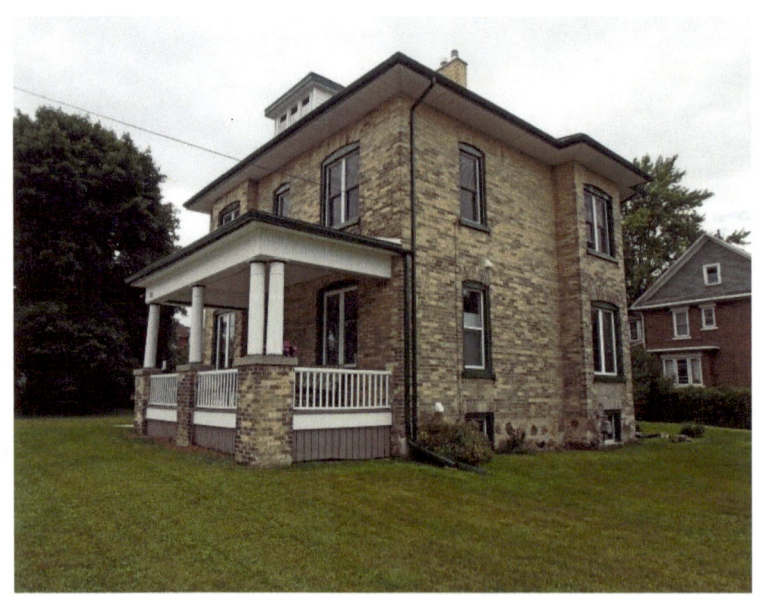

185 Jane Street – Italianate, dormer in attic

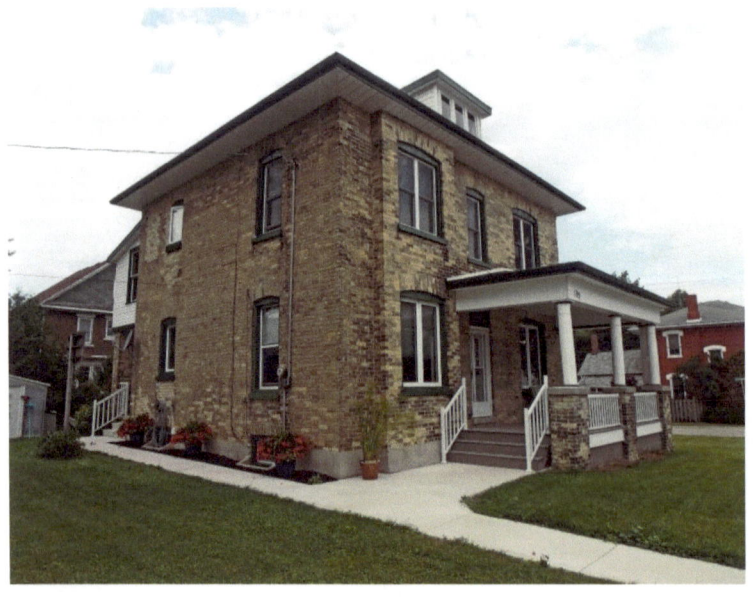

Architectural Terms

Brackets: a decorative or weight-bearing structural element which forms a right angle with one side against a wall and the other under a projecting surface such as an eave or roof. Example: 555 King Street	
Cornice: originally the wooden overhang of the roof. With the use of stone, brick, iron and steel, the cornice is any projecting shelf at the top of a ceiling or roof. They can be very decorative. Example: 350 Main Street	
Dentil Moulding: an even series of rectangles used as ornamental decoration in cornices. Example: Main Street downtown	
Dichromatic brickwork: the use of two colours of brick, tile or slate to decorate a façade. Example: Main Street	
Dormer: (French for "sleep") a gable end window that pierces through the plane of a sloping roof surface to create usable space in the top floor or attic of a building by adding headroom. Example: 555 King Street	
Fretwork: interlaced decorative design resembling a bracket Example: Bell Street	

Gable: the triangular portion of a wall between the edges of a sloping roof. Example: 520 Main Street	
Hipped Roof: a roof where all sides slope downwards to the walls with no gables. Example: 325 Main Street	
Iron Cresting: A decorative ornament along the top of a roof. Iron cresting was popular in the Baroque era and also in Italianate, Victorian, Second Empire and Queen Anne styles of architecture. Example: 620 King Street	
Keystones and Voussoirs: a voussoir is a wedge-shaped element used in building an arch. A keystone is the central stone that locks all the stones into position, allowing the arch to bear weight. A keystone is often enlarged and embellished. Example: Main Street	
Lancet Window: a tall, narrow window with a pointed arch at its top. Example: St. James Anglican Church	

Mansard Roof: This style was popularized by Francois Mansart (1598-1666), an accomplished architect of the French Baroque period and especially fashionable during the Second French Empire (1852-1870). This roof is almost flat on the top section, with two slopes on each of its sides with the lower slope at a steeper angle than the upper and having dormer windows. Example: Main Street	
Pediment: a triangular section above the horizontal structure (entablature), typically supported by columns. The inside of the triangle is called the tympanum. Example: 260 Queen Street	
Quoin: masonry blocks at the corner of a wall, often a decorative feature, usually larger or of a different colour than the rest of the wall. Example: Main Street	
Turret: a small tower that projects from the wall of a building. Example: 325 William Street	
Vergeboard and Finial: also called bargeboards – hang from the projecting end of a roof and are often elaborately carved and ornamented. **Finial:** ornament added to the top of a gable, pinnacle, canopy or spire – a Gothic element. Example: Yonge Street	

Edwardian, 1900-1930 – This style bridges the ornate and elaborate styles of the Victorian era and the simplified styles of the 20th century. Balanced facades, simple roof lines, dormer windows, large front porches, and smooth brick surfaces are its characteristics. Example: Main Street	
Gothic Revival, 1830-1890 – These decorative buildings have sharply-pitched gables with highly detailed vergeboards, pointed-arch window openings, and dichromatic brickwork. It is a common style in Ontario. Example: 135 Henry Street	
Italianate, 1850-1900 – It has wide-bracketed eaves, belvederes, wrap-around verandahs. Example: 115 Henry Street	
Queen Anne, 1885-1900 – This style is distinguished by an irregular outline featuring a combination of an offset tower, broad gables, projecting two-storey bays, verandahs, multi-sloped roofs, and tall, decorative chimneys. A mixture of brick and wood is common. Windows often have one large single-paned bottom sash and small panes in the upper sash. Example: 325 William Street	
Second Empire, 1860-1880 – The mansard roof is the most noteworthy feature of this style and is evidence of the French origins. Projecting central towers and one or two-storey bays can also be present. Example: Main Street downtown